Artificial Intelligence and the Rule of Law

Artificial intelligence is an important driving force of the new round of technological revolution and industrial change. Artificial intelligence and blockchain have risen to the level of national policy. While the rapid development of AI brings convenience to people's lives, it also poses challenges to global changes and the development of human society, social governance and legal regulation, such as the leakage of personal privacy, frequent data security problems, and prejudice and discrimination caused by algorithms. AI is profoundly changing the world, and it is necessary to think about how to promote the construction of responsible AI from the perspective of global governance in the future.

In response to these issues, this series aims to explore and study the new situations and new issues at the intersection of AI, law and political science all over the world, to provide a legal basis for the development of AI-related frontier fields and to limit the development of AI within the framework of law to promote the harmonious and orderly construction of AI and legal systems. Based on the above purpose, this series is selected and integrated with multidisciplinary strengths to strengthen the research on legal, ethical, and social issues related to AI, focusing on laws, regulations, institutional systems, and ethics for the healthy development of AI. The authors of this series are all top authoritative experts and scholars in AI, law, political science, and other disciplines in China, and they have already made considerable achievements and social reputations in this field of research.

This series has a clear awareness of the problem and proposes specific solutions for the implementation and implementation of AI governance from a multidisciplinary and multidisciplinary perspective, covering AI, blockchain, algorithms, digital currency and other specific segments closely related to law, with cutting-edge, academic and theoretical value.

Wei Liu

Computational Antitrust

Springer

Wei Liu
State Key Laboratory of Multimodel Artificial Intelligence Systems
Institute of Automation, Chinese Academy of Sciences
Beijing, Beijing, China

ISSN 2731-6238 ISSN 2731-6246 (electronic)
Artificial Intelligence and the Rule of Law
ISBN 978-981-95-5036-4 ISBN 978-981-95-5037-1 (eBook)
https://doi.org/10.1007/978-981-95-5037-1

This work was supported by National Key Research and Development Program of China (No.2022YFC3321003).

This Springer imprint is published by the registered company Springer Nature Singapore Pte Ltd.
The registered company address is: 152 Beach Road, #21-01/04 Gateway East, Singapore 189721, Singapore

To my parents, for teaching me integrity;
to my mentors, for challenging my thinking;
and to the next generation of researchers,
who will reshape antitrust for the
algorithmic age.

Foreword

As digital platforms continue to reshape the foundations of global commerce, regulators and scholars alike are being confronted with novel and complex forms of monopolistic behavior. Traditional antitrust tools, developed in the industrial era, are increasingly strained in their attempts to interpret and intervene in algorithmic markets, data-driven pricing schemes, and platform-mediated competition. In this context, *Computational Antitrust* offers a timely, interdisciplinary, and deeply informed response to these emerging challenges.

This volume explores the global evolution of antitrust frameworks, the limitations of traditional legal doctrines in the face of digital transformation, and the promise of computational techniques—ranging from machine learning to system-level simulation—for modernizing competition policy. Chapters traverse legal history, economic theory, artificial intelligence, and empirical case studies, culminating in the construction of intelligent regulatory systems for detecting, assessing, and anticipating monopolistic risks.

What makes this work particularly impactful is its integration of legal, economic, and technical perspectives into a coherent and forward-looking framework. By blending rigorous theoretical analysis with practical system design, it speaks to a broad audience—including policy makers, legal scholars, competition economists, and data scientists.

In an era where monopolistic power is increasingly coded in algorithms and scaled through platforms, this book is not only a contribution to the academic literature, but a necessary toolkit for the next generation of antitrust enforcement.

The Institute for Data Law, China University of Political Science and Law, Beijing, China
November 3, 2025

Jianzhong Shi

Preface

This monograph is situated at the confluence of antitrust theory, digital economy policy, and computational regulation. It undertakes a critical, systematic, and forward-looking examination of how monopolistic behavior evolves in the platform-based digital environment and how legal frameworks, both traditional and emergent, respond to these changes. Against the backdrop of accelerating digitization, algorithmic governance, and cross-border market integration, the study reconsiders foundational antitrust principles while proposing novel approaches informed by data science and artificial intelligence.

The digital economy, characterized by platform intermediation, data-driven value creation, and network-based competition, poses significant challenges to classical antitrust doctrines. Traditional legal frameworks grounded in static market definitions, price/output analysis, and firm-centric models of dominance are increasingly inadequate to address the complexities introduced by dynamic pricing algorithms, personalized recommendation systems, and multi-sided markets. This study interrogates such inadequacies and seeks to establish an enriched conceptual and regulatory framework for antitrust governance in the digital era.

This work integrates insights from law, economics, and computational methods. It provides a historical analysis of the development of antitrust law in major jurisdictions, evaluates the economic and legal implications of price discrimination enabled by big data, and elaborates a model for risk-based assessment of monopolistic behavior in platform enterprises. A central contribution of the study lies in its formulation of a multi-tiered antitrust risk evaluation system that quantifies behavioral risks across structural, conduct-based, and welfare-impact dimensions. This framework contributes to both academic theory-building and practical enforcement strategy design.

Particular attention is given to the emergence of computational antitrust—a new frontier in competition regulation that leverages artificial intelligence and machine learning tools to detect, model, and mitigate anti-competitive conduct. By operationalizing algorithmic techniques for identifying discriminatory pricing patterns in digital markets, this study advances a methodologically innovative and policy-relevant model for ex-ante regulation.

The research also addresses broader normative concerns, including market fairness, consumer autonomy, and the transparency of algorithmic decision-making. It emphasizes the importance of regulatory adaptation in preserving the competitive order in digital economies.

The present volume is intended to serve as a reference for graduate students, early-career researchers, and professionals engaged in the domains of competition law, digital economy regulation, and computational social science. The analytical frameworks and empirical findings presented herein are the result of extensive interdisciplinary research conducted by the authors over recent years. We hope that this work will contribute meaningfully to both the academic study and practical application of modern antitrust strategies, particularly in relation to digital platforms, algorithmic governance, and data-driven market behavior.

Despite our best efforts to ensure rigor, comprehensiveness, and clarity, the breadth and complexity of the subject matter inevitably mean that certain conceptual oversights or technical inaccuracies may remain. We sincerely welcome constructive feedback, critical commentary, and scholarly dialogue from readers, which we regard as invaluable for the continued refinement of this work and for the advancement of research in this evolving field.

Beijing, China
August 2, 2025

Wei Liu

Acknowledgments

This book is the result of several years of interdisciplinary research and collaboration at the intersection of law, economics, and computational science. We would like to express our sincere gratitude to the institutions and individuals whose support made this work possible.

First and foremost, we thank the Ministry of Science and Technology and the National Natural Science Foundation of China for supporting the foundational research projects that underpinned this book. We are also grateful to the Multimodal Artificial Intelligence Systems Laboratory at the Institute of Automation, Chinese Academy of Sciences, for providing the computational infrastructure and research environment necessary for our work.

We extend special thanks to Professor Weiming Hu for his invaluable mentorship and guidance throughout the development of this project, and to our collaborators from State Administration for Market Regulation Competition Policy and Evaluation Center, China University of Political Science and Law and East China University of Political Science and Law for their insightful discussions on antitrust theory and computational law. We thank our research interns Ziheng Feng, Chao Jiao, and Yipeng Wang for their dedicated contributions to the implementation of algorithmic components in this project.

We also acknowledge the support of the editorial team at Springer for their professional assistance during the preparation of this manuscript.

Finally, we thank our families for their unwavering encouragement and understanding throughout the research and writing process.

Beijing China
August 2, 2025

Wei Liu

Contents

Contributors

Ning Du School of Intellectual Property, East China University of Political Science and Law, Shanghai, China

Qing Gao School of Juris Master, China University of Political Science and Law, Beijing, China

Weiming Hu State Key Laboratory of Multimodal Artificial Intelligence Systems, Institute of Automation, Chinese Academy of Sciences, Beijing, China

Bing Li State Key Laboratory of Multimodal Artificial Intelligence Systems, Institute of Automation, Chinese Academy of Sciences, Beijing, China

Wei Liu State Key Laboratory of Multimodal Artificial Intelligence Systems, Institute of Automation, Chinese Academy of Sciences, Beijing, China

Jiying Wu State Administration for Market Regulation Competition Policy and Evaluation Center, Beijing, China

Li Yang State Key Laboratory of Multimodal Artificial Intelligence Systems, Institute of Automation, Chinese Academy of Sciences, Beijing, China

Abbreviations

AI	Artificial Intelligence
AML	Anti-Monopoly Law
AMSA	Administration of the People's Republic of China
APEC	Asia-Pacific Economic Cooperation
API	application programming interface
AR	augmented reality
BCAs	bilateral cooperation agreements
BDDP	big data-driven discriminatory pricing
CAICT	China Academy of Information and Communications Technology
CPFA	Policy Framework Agreement
CRM	customer relationship management
CV	Computer Vision
DL	Deep Learning
DNNs	Deep neural networks
DPMC	Dual Pricing Model Clustering
DT	Decision tree
EC	European Commission
ERP	Enterprise resource planning
EU	European Union
FN	False Negatives
FP	False Positives
FTC	Federal Trade Commission
GAMS	General Administration of Market Supervision
GNNs	Graph neural networks
HHI	Herfindahl-Hirschman Index
ICN	International Competition Network
ICT	Information and communication technologies
IE	Internet Explorer
ILSVRC	ImageNet Large Scale Visual Recognition Challenge
KFTC	Korea Fair Trade Commission
LACCF	Latin American and Caribbean Competition Forum

LLMs	large language models
LoRA	Low-Rank Adaptation
M&A	Merger and acquisition
ML	Machine Learning
MOUs	Memorandums of understanding
MSE	Mean Squared Error
NAFTA	North American Free Trade Agreement
NER	Named entity recognition
NLP	Natural Language Processing
OECD	Organisation for Economic Co-operation and Development
PC	Personal computer
PCA	Principal Component Analysis
SEP	Standard-essential patent
TF	True Negatives
TP	True Positives
UNCTAD	United Nations Conference on Trade and Development
VR	Virtual reality
WTO	World Trade Organization

Chapter 1
Global History and Development of Antitrust

Abstract This chapter offers a comprehensive, policy-oriented survey of the global history and development of antitrust. It begins by clarifying core concepts—monopoly, mechanisms of dominance, and market implications—and traces the emergence of modern competition law from the late nineteenth century to contemporary frameworks across the United States, Europe, and Asia. Building on this historical foundation, the chapter examines institutional architectures for cross-border cooperation, including bilateral agreements, regional arrangements, and multilateral fora that enable information sharing, coordinated remedies, and converging enforcement practices.

To ground the discussion, we analyze representative cases that shaped doctrine and policy: U.S. conduct and platform cases, EU actions at the interface of SEPs and competition, and emblematic Asian matters in e-commerce and messaging ecosystems. These case studies illuminate recurring issues—bundling, self preferencing, exclusionary contracting, data advantages, and privacy-competition interactions—and how legal standards adapt as technology and markets evolve.

The chapter then turns to the digital economy's distinctive challenges: data-driven market power, multisided network effects, ecosystem competition, and cross-border integration that strains traditional tools for defining markets and assessing power. In response, we outline a modernisation agenda: clearer treatment of data monopolies, dynamic market assessment beyond static shares, enhanced international and cross sectoral coordination, and the rise of "computational antitrust" that leverages data analytics and algorithmic audits to support timely, evidence-based decisions. The chapter closes with practical pathways for regulators and policymakers to safeguard contestability and innovation while protecting consumer welfare in increasingly digital and globally interconnected markets.

Keywords Antitrust law · Competition policy · Monopoly and market power · Digital economy · Platform economy · Data monopoly · Network effects · Bilateral/multisided markets · International cooperation · Merger control ·

W. Liu, *Computational Antitrust*, Artificial Intelligence and the Rule of Law,
https://doi.org/10.1007/978-981-95-5037-1_1

Standard-essential patents (SEPs) · Algorithmic transparency · Computational antitrust · Cross-border enforcement · Consumer welfare

1.1 The Origins and Evolution of Antitrust Law

1.1.1 Monopolies: Definitions, Mechanisms and Market Impacts

Monopoly, usually defined as the dominance of a single firm or a small number of firms in a given market, creates the ability to exercise substantial control over the market by controlling production, sales, access to resources or other means. This control allows the monopolist to manipulate prices and restrict competition to a certain extent and to maintain significant influence in the market, resulting in interference with the free operation of market supply and demand, and thus creating a state of market exclusivity.

The causes of monopoly formation are complex and multifaceted, encompassing but not limited to the following scenarios. First, tacit coordination or collusion among oligopolistic firms may lead to joint actions aimed at excluding competitors. Second, cross-sector operations enable firms to consolidate their monopolistic positions by leveraging influence across multiple markets [1]. Third, government protectionism, in the form of laws or policies, can confer competitive advantages on specific firms. Fourth, a firm may establish dominance through proprietary technologies or continuous innovation. Fifth, natural monopolies may arise from economies of scale—where industries such as water supply, electricity, natural gas, and railways require extremely high fixed costs but incur low marginal costs, making large-scale production by a single firm more efficient than competition among multiple firms. In conclude, monopolistic phenomena can be further categorized into five main types: scale-based monopoly, technology-driven monopoly, administrative monopoly, natural monopoly, and strategic monopoly. Each type emerges from distinct structural conditions and operates through specific mechanisms of influence.

Although monopolistic behaviour and free competition may appear to be opposites, they can actually coexist to some extent. Monopolies do not completely eliminate the competitive element in the market, but rather override free competition through their dominant position. Therefore, when analysing the impact of monopolies on the market, we need to take a dialectical view, looking at both their potential positive effects and their possible negative consequences.

From the perspective of positive impact, monopolists, because of their market size, are often able to realise economies of scale and improve the overall efficiency of the market by reducing production costs. For example, in certain high-technology industries, the resources and capabilities of a monopolist enable it to invest huge amounts of money in research and development and innovation, promoting technological progress and industrial upgrading. In addition, monopolists also have the ability to stabilize the market, which can, to a certain extent, avoid drastic fluctuations in the market and ensure the continuous and stable operation of the market.

However, the negative effects of monopolistic behavior cannot be ignored. Monopolies tend to weaken market competition by preventing other competitors from entering the market, resulting in a lack of effective competitive pressure in the market. In such an environment, the quality of products and services may gradually deteriorate, consumers' room for choice is restricted, and the overall vigour of market innovation is consequently weakened. In the long run, the monopolist may lack the incentive to improve its products or services due to the lack of competitive challenges, which in turn leads to the market lagging behind the demand for technological advancement [2]. The market may lag behind the demand for technological advances [2].

In this context, the primary purpose of antitrust legislation is to prevent and prohibit monopolists from abusing their dominant market positions. By enforcing antitrust regulations, unfair monopolistic practices can be effectively curbed, thereby safeguarding fair competition, protecting consumer interests, and fostering a healthy development of the market. The existence of an antitrust legal framework not only preserves the integrity of free market competition but also serves as a vital mechanism for ensuring innovation dynamics and enhancing consumer welfare.

1.1.2 Historical Origins and Core Principles of Antitrust Law

The origin and development of antitrust law has been a complex process spanning many centuries and a wide geographic area, with the core objective of preventing monopolistic and anticompetitive behaviour in the marketplace, thereby protecting the interests of consumers and preserving healthy competition in the marketplace. The germ of antitrust thinking can be traced back to the Late Middle Ages and the Renaissance, when commercial regulations began to attempt to limit the control and pricing power of guilds in the marketplace. The origins of modern antitrust law, however, are largely rooted in the industrialisation process of the late nineteenth and early twentieth centuries.

With the advance of the Industrial Revolution in the late nineteenth century, the United States economy underwent unprecedented changes. Large-scale factories and multinational enterprises rose rapidly, and these large enterprises gradually monopolised the market through mergers and acquisitions, leading to a drastic weakening of competition, manipulation of market prices and damage to consumer interests. The worsening monopoly phenomenon triggered strong social discontent, and public opinion gradually protested against the behaviour of these giant enterprises. The government and legislators have begun to realise that allowing this monopolistic trend to continue may have far-reaching negative impacts on the economy and society. As a result, there is a growing clamour to curb monopolies and maintain the order of market competition.

Against this background, the United States Congress passed the Sherman Antitrust Act in 1890, the world's first comprehensive antitrust law, marking the formal establishment of the modern antitrust law system. The core objective of the Sherman Act was to prohibit companies from organising themselves through trusts in order to restrict competition and manipulate the market. The Act not only pioneered the antitrust law system in the United States, but also provided a model for antitrust legislation in countries around the world.

The formulation of antitrust law aims to protect market competition by preventing and curbing monopolistic behavior, thereby ensuring a sufficient level of competition in the marketplace. This, in turn, encourages enterprises to innovate continuously and improve the quality of their products and services. Over the course of the development and enforcement of antitrust law, a series of fundamental principles have gradually emerged and become well-established.

One such principle is the focus on the anticompetitive effects of conduct. According to the foundational doctrines of U.S. antitrust law, anticompetitive effects can be classified into two distinct categories: collusive effects and exclusionary effects. The former refers to situations where businesses coordinate with competitors through practices such as price fixing, output restrictions, market allocation, or collective boycotts, resulting in prices being raised above competitive levels or output reduced below them. The latter involves practices like exclusive dealing, refusal to deal, tying arrangements, predatory pricing, and discriminatory treatment aimed at excluding rivals, thereby similarly distorting price and output outcomes in the market. In addition, European competition law introduces the concept of exploitative abuse, where a dominant firm harms trading partners or consumers through unfair trading arrangements. The most common forms of such abuse under EU law include excessive pricing and price discrimination.

Another guiding principle is the integration of international standards with domestic realities. Antitrust legislation must adhere to globally recognized legal norms while adapting to the specific characteristics of the national market and economy, ensuring effective domestic market regulation within the context of globalization. Furthermore, the law must balance generality and specificity—providing broad definitions to cover a wide array of monopolistic practices, while also listing representative examples to offer clear legal guidance. The combination of procedural and substantive rules is also critical: antitrust law not only regulates the substance of monopolistic behavior but also emphasizes procedural justice, ensuring transparency, fairness, and due process in enforcement.

Protecting national economic interests is another important principle. Antitrust law should safeguard the core interests of the domestic economy, particularly in the face of international competition, by preventing unfair external shocks to local markets and enterprises. Additionally, the principle of prioritizing efficiency plays a crucial role. While promoting fairness, antitrust law must also guard against the harm monopolies pose to market efficiency and ensure that regulatory interventions do not themselves hinder effective market functioning.

In light of China's specific market characteristics, Chinese antitrust law places special emphasis on several additional principles. These include building a unified, open, competitive, and well-ordered market system by eliminating market barriers through legislation and fostering the development of a nationwide integrated market. Moreover, it upholds the balance between protecting economic freedoms and preserving necessary governmental oversight and regulation, ensuring both individual and corporate liberties and the integrity of market order.

Together, these principles form the foundation of antitrust law, providing both theoretical and practical guidance for its enforcement and ensuring the healthy development of markets under fair and competitive conditions.

1.1.3 Historical Development of Antitrust Laws in Major Countries and Regions Around the World

The development of antitrust law has undergone a unique process in different regions at different times, as shown in Fig. 1.1. The United States, as the forerunner of antitrust law, has gone through several stages of refinement and strengthening since the passage of the Sherman Antitrust Act in 1890, culminating in the formation of a complex and robust body of law. Europe, on the other hand, has gradually centralised and modernised since World War II, especially in the late twentieth century when several important statutes were passed to strengthen the regulation of multinational enterprises. Asian countries, such as Japan and China, have also gradually developed their respective antitrust law systems in different historical contexts, with Japan stepping up enforcement in the post-World War II period and China formally enforcing its own antitrust law in 2008, marking an important advance in this area.

(1) United States of America first

- **Early legislative phase** (1890): This phase marks the origins of antitrust law in the United States and refers primarily to the passage of the Sherman Antitrust Act.
- **Early Perfection Stage** (1914): After the Sherman Act, the passage of the Clayton Antitrust Act and the Tefft-Hartley Act further improved the antitrust legal system. These Acts established the Federal Trade Commission and the Antitrust Division of the United States Department of Justice, which strengthened the regulation and enforcement of monopolistic practices.
- **Intermediate strengthening phase** (1930s to 1950s): During the period from the 1930s to the 1950s, antitrust efforts against monopolistic behaviour in the United States continued to strengthen, with the emergence of a series of laws and cases, such as the Robinson-Patman Act and the Clayton-Cutler Act. These laws strengthened the regulation of unfair competition and anti-competitive behaviour and further improved the antitrust legal system.
- **Later stage of refinement and adjustment** (1960s to present): From the 1960s to present, the U.S. antitrust law continues to develop and improve, including revisions and adjustments to the law to adapt to changes in the economy and market. At the same time, with the accumulation of research and practical experi-

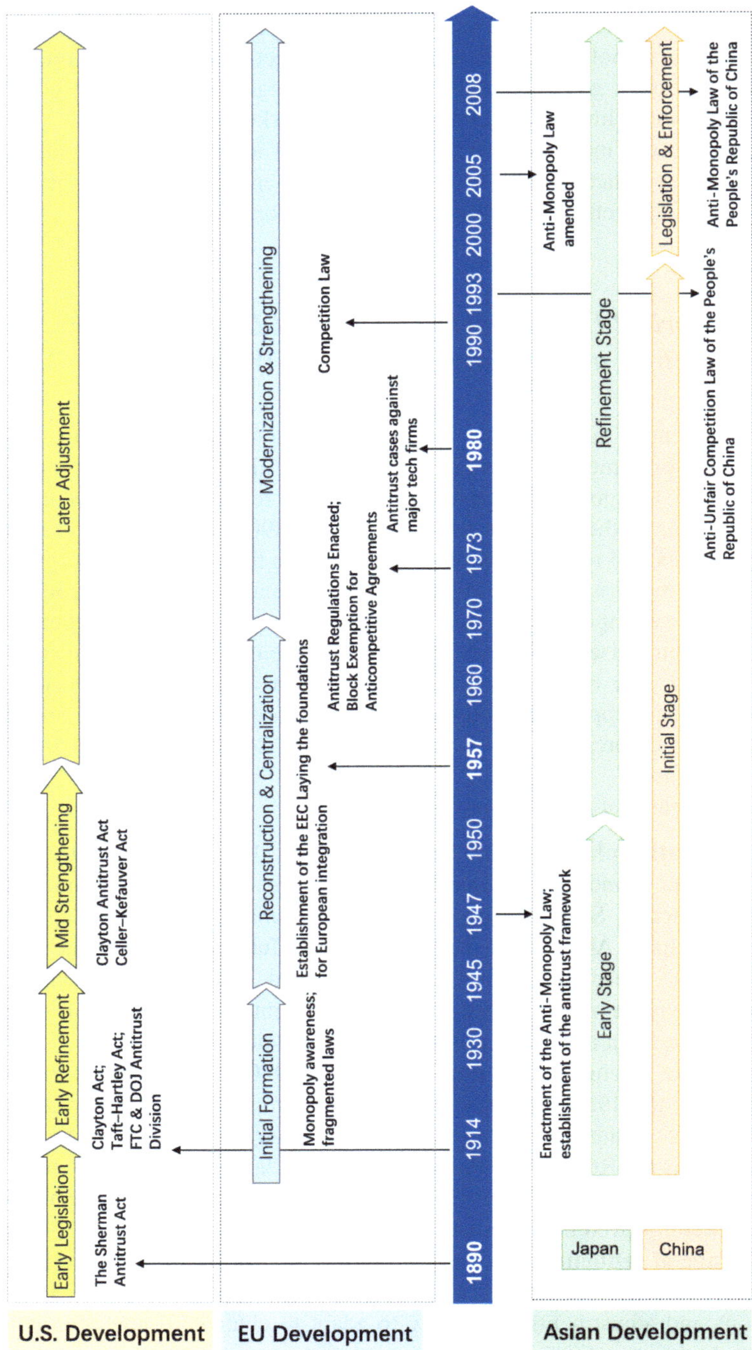

Fig. 1.1 Overview of global antitrust developments

ence in antitrust law, the U.S. has continuously reflected on and adjusted its antitrust policies and enforcement practices [3].

(2) Developments in Europe

- **Early formative stage** (early twentieth century to 1945): In the early twentieth century, European countries began to realise the negative impact of monopolistic practices on the economy, but anti-trust legislation was still fragmented and imperfect. The First World War and the post-war turmoil also affected the development of antitrust law.
- **-Stage of reconstruction and centralisation** (1945–1970s): After the end of the Second World War, European countries began to carry out economic reconstruction, and at the same time, the problem of monopolies arose. In 1957, the European Economic Community (EEC) was established, laying the foundation for European integration. Thereafter, the EEC began to take measures to restrict monopolies and promote fair competition, such as anti-monopoly actions through legal documents such as the Treaty of Rome.
- **Modernisation and Strengthening Phase.** Pursuant to Council Regulation No. 19/65/EEC (the 1965 Empowerment Regulation), the Council authorized the European Commission to issue block exemption regulations specifying types of agreements that are presumed to satisfy the exemption criteria set out in Article 101(3) of the Treaty on the Functioning of the European Union (TFEU). Acting under this authority, the Commission has introduced multiple block exemptions, including several relating to vertical agreements.

In the 1980s, the European Commission began to take more aggressive antitrust action, such as antitrust investigations and sanctions against large technology companies such as Microsoft and IBM.

In 1990, the European Union (EU) adopted the Antitrust Regulation, which further strengthened the regulation of monopolies and anti-competitive behaviour.

From the 2000s to the present, the European Commission has continued to carry out antitrust investigations and sanctions, for example against technology giants such as Google and Apple.

(3) Follow-up in Asia

In the course of studying the stages of antitrust law development in Asia, we have mainly used representative Asian countries—Japan and China—as references.

- Development of antimonopoly law in Japan:

Early stage (early to mid-twentieth century): Japan began to realise the negative impact of monopolistic practices on the economy in the early twentieth century, but the enactment of antimonopoly laws lagged behind. in 1947, the Antimonopoly Law was enacted, which established a legal framework for antimonopoly, but there were some limitations in its practical implementation.

Strengthening and Improvement Stage (Late twentieth Century to Present): After the 1990s, with the development of the Japanese economy and changes in the international market, the Japanese government strengthened the enforcement of the antimonopoly law and imposed stricter regulations on acts such as cartels and abuse of dominant position in the market.In 2005, the Antimonopoly Law was amended to strengthen the penalties for monopolistic acts and unfair competition, and to established a stricter review system.

– Development of China's anti-monopoly law:

Early stage (early to late twentieth century): With the establishment of China's socialist market economic system, the Chinese Government began to pay attention to anti-monopoly construction. The earliest prescriptive document on anti-monopoly law in China was the Provisional Provisions on the Promotion of Economic Unions issued by the State Council in July 1980, which proposed to "break regional blockades and sectoral divisions". The second is the Interim Provisions on the Development and Protection of Socialist Competition issued by the State Council in October 1980, which states that "in economic activities, except for products designated by the State to be operated exclusively by the relevant departments or units, no other products can be monopolised and monopolistic operations can be carried out". In 1986, the State Council issued the Regulations on Deepening Enterprise Reform and Enhancing Enterprise Vitality, which stipulated that "in the same industry, there should generally be no exclusive monopoly enterprise groups, so as to facilitate the development of competition and promote technological advancement"; and in 1987, the State Council issued the Regulations on Price Administration and Regulations on the Administration of Advertisements, which also stipulated against price monopoly respectively. In 1989, the State Reform Commission and other departments jointly issued the Interim Measures on Enterprise Mergers, which made the prevention of monopoly a basic principle of enterprise mergers.The Law of the People's Republic of China Against Unfair Competition (hereinafter referred to as the "Anti-Unfair Competition Law"), which was adopted in 1993, also prohibits several specific behaviours that restrict competition and explicitly provides for the prevention of monopoly in order to facilitate competition and promote technological advancement. and clearly stipulates the corresponding legal liabilities. In December of the same year, the State Administration for Industry and Commerce (SAIC) issued the Provisions on Prohibiting Public Enterprises from Restricting Competition, which crystallised the provisions on monopoly in the Anti-Unfair Competition Law, and became a more systematic anti-monopoly regulation in China, which was once referred to as "the anti-monopoly law at this stage".

Legislation and Law Enforcement Phase (early twenty-first century to present): In 2008, the Anti-Monopoly Law of the People's Republic of China was formally implemented, making it the first anti-monopoly law in China's history. The law stipulates the basic principles and prohibited behaviours of anti-monopoly, establishes an anti-monopoly enforcement agency, and strengthens the supervision and penalties of monopoly behaviours [4].Afterwards, China's antitrust legal system has undergone significant refinement through multiple amendments, with the framework becoming increasingly comprehensive. For instance, the 2022 revision of the Anti-Monopoly Law (AML) introduced a critical provision under Article 19, which explicitly prohibits business operators from "organizing or facilitating other operators to reach monopoly agreements." This amendment addressed a longstanding regulatory gap while reinforcing the "foundational status of competition policy" in China's market governance.

To enhance enforcement precision, antitrust authorities have issued supporting regulations and guidelines, clarifying regulatory standards in specialized areas such as standard-essential patents (SEPs) and the platform economy. Notably, China released the world's first "Anti-Monopoly Guidelines on Standard-Essential Patents," establishing a coordinated approach to balancing intellectual property rights and antitrust compliance.

1.2 Framework for International Anti-Monopoly Cooperation

With the development of economic globalisation, the space for economic activities of market entities is no longer limited to a certain country or region, and the dependence of national and regional markets on each other is increasing; globalisation has also made it easier for transnational corporations to transfer funds, resources and profits among several countries, which has made it more difficult for countries to combat monopoly unilaterally, and therefore countries and regions need international cooperation in antimonopoly. At present, the field of antitrust international cooperation presents three kinds of cooperation mechanisms: bilateral, regional and multilateral, each with its own characteristics and complementary to the other [5]. The international co-operation in the field of antimonopoly is currently presented as bilateral, regional and multilateral co-operation mechanisms, each with its own characteristics and complementing the other [5].

1.2.1 The Role of Bilateral Cooperation Mechanisms in Antimonopoly Enforcement

Bilateral cooperation is the starting point for international antitrust law cooperation until it becomes integrated. The model of bilateral cooperation includes both informal cooperation between antitrust enforcement agencies based on the framework of their respective domestic laws, as well as the signing of memorandums of understanding (MOUs) or formal bilateral cooperation agreements (BCAs) between two countries. Unlike regional and multilateral co-operation agreements, bilateral co-operation agreements are generally specialised competition co-operation treaties, i.e., the content of the treaty focuses on competition law issues. There are currently several antitrust organisations or agreements in the form of international bilateral cooperation:

Competition Policy Framework Agreement (CPFA) This is an agreement under the World Trade Organisation (WTO) to promote coordination and cooperation in competition policy among member countries.

The Intel antitrust security review is a representative case related to this agreement. Not satisfied with its dominant position in the chip market, Intel exerted tremendous pressure on some major computer manufacturers and retailers in Europe to use or prioritise the use of Intel's chips only and not use or restrict the use of AMD's chips, in order to exclude and suppress AMD and hinder its development in the chip market. In this incident, the EU cooperated with the United States Federal Trade Commission (FTC), the European Competition Commission (EC) and other antitrust enforcement agencies on the basis of the competition policy framework to regulate and sanction Intel's abuse of market monopoly position through information sharing and other means.

Bilateral Antimonopoly Agreements Bilateral antimonopoly agreements signed between countries to strengthen the regulation and sanctioning of monopolistic behaviour of TNCs.

The most representative incident related to this is the Microsoft antitrust case. In 1998, the U.S. Department of Justice filed an antitrust lawsuit against Microsoft, alleging that Microsoft had abused its monopoly on the Windows operating system, hindering competition from other companies and violating the U.S. antitrust laws, and in 2004, the European Competition Commission (EC) filed an antitrust lawsuit against Microsoft, alleging that it had damaged competition by bundling its products, refusing to undermine competition by bundling products, refusing to provide technical information to competitors, and so on. As a result, the antitrust enforcement agencies of the United States and the European Union cooperated under a bilateral antitrust agreement, and the case had a far-reaching impact on the competitive landscape of the global technology industry.

Competition Enforcement Cooperation Agreement (Antitrust Enforcement Cooperation Agreement) A cooperation agreement signed between competition enforcement agencies of two or more countries to strengthen the fight against transnational monopolistic behaviour. These agreements usually include joint investigations, exchange of evidence, coordination of actions, etc., and help to improve the efficiency and cost-effectiveness of antitrust actions.

One of the representative cases of relevance is the cooperation case between FedEx and the United States Federal Trade Commission (FTC). In this case, FedEx was charged for supplying drugs to a number of Internet pharmacies and online pharmacies in violation of federal law, for conduct that included, among other things, sending controlled substances to customers who did not hold a legitimate prescription. In the course of the investigation, the US FTC cooperated with FedEx and signed a competition enforcement cooperation agreement, an event that also underscores the importance of cooperation and communication between antitrust law enforcement agencies and businesses.

International Competition Network (ICN) ICN is an international organisation of competition law enforcement agencies, which aims to promote cooperation and exchanges among national competition law enforcement agencies, and to enhance the efficiency and consistency of competition policies, enforcement and procedures. ICN does not make rules, but provides a forum where members can Discuss and share best practices. ICN members also enhance information sharing, policy coordination and experience exchange by holding annual meetings, organising working groups and issuing guidance documents, which help to enhance the effectiveness of global antitrust cooperation. ICN is usually not directly involved in investigating and adjudicating individual cases, but the guidance documents it designates and the sharing of experience it provides have a significant impact on global antitrust cooperation.

As bilateral cooperation agreements are cooperation arrangements that specifically address competition issues and are able to delve into specific aspects and issues in the antimonopoly process of concentration of operators, rather than just principles and general provisions, they have obvious advantages in terms of operability and have become the main and widely adopted model of antimonopoly cooperation in major market economies.

1.2.2 Mechanisms and Practices of Regional Antimonopoly Cooperation

Regional cooperation mechanisms in antitrust refer to a framework of cooperation between competition enforcement agencies of multiple countries or regions within a given geographical area, aimed at strengthening the regulation and combating of cross-border monopolistic behaviour. There are currently several antitrust organisations or agreements in the form of international bilateral cooperation:

There are several types of organisations or agreements in the form of international antitrust regional cooperation, each of which plays an important role in strengthening the regulation and combating of cross-border monopolistic practices and has achieved certain results:

European Commission (EC) In the context of antitrust enforcement within the European Union, the European Commission (EC), as one of the Union's key executive bodies, plays a central role in implementing competition policy and ensuring compliance with antitrust regulations. Through the issuance of antitrust guidelines, the investigation of monopolistic practices, and the imposition of penalties, the EC has actively safeguarded fair competition within the internal market, thereby contributing to the broader development of the European economy. A particularly representative example of the EC's antitrust actions lies in its multiple investigations into Google. These cases have focused on Google's conduct in areas such as search result rankings, the online advertising market, and mobile operating systems, highlighting the EC's commitment to addressing potential abuses of market dominance in the digital economy.

North American Free Trade Agreement (NAFTA) NAFTA is a free trade agreement in North America that includes the United States, Canada and Mexico.NAFTA has strengthened antitrust co-operation in North America through the development of a common competition policy framework and enforcement mechanisms, promoting fair competition and economic integration in the region's internal markets.

Asia-Pacific Economic Cooperation (APEC) APEC is an economic cooperation organisation in the Asia-Pacific region that aims to promote economic cooperation and trade liberalisation among its member countries. APEC itself is not directly involved in specific incidents of antitrust conduct, but rather strengthens antitrust cooperation in the Asia-Pacific region through the issuance of guidance documents on competition policy, the organisation of workshops and training activities, etc., APEC has strengthened antitrust cooperation in the Asia-Pacific region and promoted economic development and cooperation among member countries.

Latin American and Caribbean Competition Forum (LACCF) LACCF is a competition policy co-operation organisation in Latin America and the Caribbean, aiming to promote antitrust co-operation and exchange of experiences among member countries. LACCF has strengthened antitrust cooperation in the region by organising meetings, publishing research reports and cooperating in investigations, and has promoted the coordination and integrated development of competition policy.

1.2.3 Multilateral Cooperation and Global Antitrust Coordination

- **World Trade Organization (WTO)**: The WTO aims to promote the liberalisation and development of global trade through the establishment of trade rules and the settlement of trade disputes.The WTO's Agreement on Competition Policy and Antimonopoly Policy provides a framework for member countries to encourage them to formulate and enforce effective competition policy and antimonopoly laws.
- **United Nations Conference on Trade and Development (UNCTAD)**: UNCTAD is a United Nations agency dedicated to promoting trade and development in developing countries.UNCTAD provides technical assistance and policy advice to developing countries through research and publication of reports on monopoly and competition policy. UNCTAD promotes antitrust cooperation on a global scale by researching and publishing reports on monopoly and competition policy, and providing technical assistance and policy advice to developing countries.

- **Organisation for Economic Co-operation and Development (OECD)**: is an international organisation of 36 major economies working to promote economic growth, employment and development, and to improve economic and social well-being in member countries and globally.OECD's work covers a wide range of areas, including economic policy, employment, education, environment, taxation, and innovation. OECD also plays an important role in international antitrust co-operation. Although it is not directly involved in specific incidents of antitrust behaviour, it provides a framework and support for international antitrust cooperation through its Competition Committee and related studies, reports and guidance documents.

1.3 Analysis of Typical Antitrust Cases and Practical Innovation

1.3.1 Antitrust Practice in the United States: Case Studies and Institutional Reflections

Case 1: The Microsoft Monopoly Case
[Case background]

- Market context

In the 1990s, the personal computer (PC) market was in its golden age of rapid growth. With the rise of the Internet, browsers became the key portal for users to access the Internet. Microsoft, as the world's largest computer software company at that time, almost monopolised the PC operating system market with its Windows operating system, which was so popular that it almost became the standard configuration for PCs.

- Microsoft's marketing strategy

When Microsoft launched the Windows 95 operating system, it decided to bundle its own Internet Explorer (IE) browser with the operating system. This strategy allowed Internet Explorer to rapidly gain market share, posing a significant threat to competitor Netscape Navigator, one of the first commercial browsers on the market and once a dominant player in the browser market. However, with the bundling of Internet Explorer, Netscape's market share declined sharply, and eventually went into decline.

- Filing of antitrust charges

The United States Government and a number of state governments believe that Microsoft has taken advantage of its dominant position in the operating system market to unfairly exclude competition in the browser market by bundling the sale of Internet Explorer. They are concerned that if such behaviour is allowed to continue, it will seriously harm competition in the market, limit innovation and ultimately harm consumers.

[Processing]

- Preliminary investigations and prosecutions

In 1997, the US Federal Trade Commission (FTC) began an investigation into Microsoft's market behaviour. However, the FTC was not able to reach a consensus on Microsoft's behaviour and eventually decided not to file a lawsuit. Subsequently, however, the U.S. Department of Justice and a number of state governments decided to act jointly to file an antitrust lawsuit against Microsoft.

- Complicated legal and technical disputes

During the trial of the case, the parties engaged in heated debates on a number of legal and technical issues. Microsoft argued that its bundled sales behavior was motivated by the need to enhance user experience and integrate product features, rather than for the purpose of excluding competition. At the same time, Microsoft also emphasised that the Windows operating system and Internet Explorer were technically tightly integrated and that separating them would harm the overall performance and user experience of the products.

For their part, the US government and state governments insisted that Microsoft's behaviour violated the antitrust laws and undermined the market environment of fair competition. They pointed out that Microsoft had improperly used its dominant position in the operating system market to suppress competition in the browser market through its bundling strategy.

- Court decisions and settlements

After several years of trial and argument, the court finally ruled that Microsoft had failed to fully comply with the antitrust laws and required Microsoft to take remedial measures. Specifically, the Court required Microsoft to separate its operating system from its Internet Explorer browser to avoid unfairly affecting competition in the browser market. In addition, Microsoft was required to disclose portions of its application programming interface (API) so that competitors could more easily develop software compatible with the Windows operating system.

However, in the course of actual enforcement, Microsoft reached a settlement agreement with the US government and state governments. Under the agreement, Microsoft agreed not to engage in similar bundled sales practices and paid a fine. At the same time, Microsoft also promised to enhance the compatibility and openness of its products to promote market competition and innovation [6].

[Impact and significance]

- Impact on the technology sector

The Microsoft monopoly case has had far-reaching implications for the global technology industry. Firstly, it has prompted enterprises to re-examine the boundaries of the use of a dominant market position. Enterprises are beginning to realise that even if they have a strong market position, they cannot abuse it to exclude competition or harm consumers. Otherwise, they will face serious legal consequences and reputational damage.

Second, the case promotes the principles of open standards and technology neutrality. With Microsoft being required to separate its operating system from its browser, the principles of open standards and technology neutrality have gradually become an important trend in the technology industry. These principles encourage companies to adopt open technology standards and interfaces to promote interoperability and compatibility between different products.

– Development of the antitrust laws

The Microsoft monopoly case also provides new ideas and directions for the development of antitrust law. Firstly, the case demonstrates the important role of antitrust law in maintaining market competition and protecting consumer interests. By punishing abuses of market dominance, the antitrust law helps to maintain a fair, transparent and competitive market environment.

Second, the case prompted the antitrust law to continuously adapt to the development of new technologies and new markets. With the rise of the digital and network economy, antitrust law needs to be more flexible in responding to the challenges posed by new technologies and new markets. For example, issues such as how to define the market boundaries of the platform economy and how to assess the impact of network effects on market competition need to be thoroughly studied and explored by the antitrust law.

– Impact on Microsoft itself

The Microsoft monopoly case has also had a far-reaching impact on Microsoft itself. Firstly, the case has caused some damage to Microsoft's market image and reputation. Microsoft's alleged abuse of its dominant market position triggered widespread controversy and criticism, resulting in a certain degree of damage to its market image.

Second, the case prompted Microsoft to strengthen its focus on market competition and compliance. In order to avoid similar legal disputes and reputational losses, Microsoft began to pay more attention to market competition and compliance issues. For example, Microsoft strengthened its investment in product compatibility and openness to enhance the market acceptance and user satisfaction of its products. At the same time, Microsoft has also strengthened the training and management of its employees to enhance their awareness and ability to respond to market competition and compliance issues.

[Insights and summary]

The Microsoft monopoly case is a classic case in the field of antitrust law, which not only reveals the potential risks and challenges of enterprises in a dominant market position, but also demonstrates the important role of antitrust law in safeguarding market competition and protecting consumer interests. Through the case, we can draw the following insights:

The double-edged sword of market dominance: Market dominance is both a competitive advantage and a source of potential risk for an enterprise. While enjoying the benefits of a dominant market position, enterprises must always be alert to potential legal risks and reputational damage.

Importance of open standards and technology neutrality: The principles of open standards and technology neutrality help promote competition and innovation in the marketplace. By adopting open technology standards and interfaces, companies can better achieve interoperability and compatibility between products, thereby improving the overall efficiency and competitiveness of the market.

Adaptability and flexibility of the antitrust law: With the continuous development of new technologies and new markets, the antitrust law needs to be constantly adapted and changed. Antimonopoly authorities need to pay close attention to market dynamics and technological development trends, and adjust and improve relevant laws, regulations and policy measures in a timely manner, in order to better safeguard market competition and protect consumer interests.

The Microsoft monopoly case is an important milestone in the field of antitrust law. It reveals the potential risks and challenges of enterprises in a dominant market position and demonstrates the important role of antitrust law in maintaining market competition and protecting consumer interests. By analysing the handling process and impact of the case, we can better understand the implementation effect and regulatory significance of the antitrust law. At the same time, the case also provides us with valuable experience and lessons to remind us to remain vigilant and compliance-conscious in future market competition and work together to maintain a fair, transparent and competitive market environment.

Case 2: Google Search Monopoly Controversy
[Case background]

- Google's market position

As the world's largest search engine company, Google has long dominated the search engine market. According to the reports of many market research institutes, Google's worldwide search engine market share far exceeds that of other competitors, forming a near-monopoly market position. This market position allows Google to have a huge voice and control in the display of search results, advertising and promotion.

- Focus of the dispute

As Google's market position has consolidated and expanded, controversy over its market behaviour has grown. The controversy focuses on the following aspects:

Search result bias: Critics have pointed out that Google may be biased in its search results by giving priority to displaying its own services or websites with which it has business partnerships, while downgrading or excluding competitors' services. Such behaviour may limit users' search choices and undermine the fairness of market competition [7].

Advertising promotion strategy: Google's AdWords advertising system allows advertisers to display adverts in search results through bidding rankings. However, there is a view that Google may be unfair in advertising promotion, such as giving more exposure to its own services or large clients at the expense of small businesses and start-ups.

Data Monopoly: As a search engine giant, Google holds a huge amount of user search data and browsing behaviour data. These data not only help Google optimise its search results and advertising and promotion strategies, but may also be used for other commercial purposes. Critics worry that Google may use these data advantages to further consolidate its market position and exclude competitors.

– Antitrust Investigations and Litigation

In view of Google's strong position in the search engine market and the controversy it has generated, antitrust agencies in several countries and regions have begun investigations into its market behaviour. At the same time, there are also competitors and consumer protection organisations filing antitrust lawsuits against Google, alleging violations of antitrust laws.

[Processing]

– Antitrust investigations

In the face of multiple challenges, Google has been repeatedly investigated by antitrust agencies in various countries. These investigations mainly centred on Google's dominant market position, whether the search results were fair, whether the advertisements were promoted fairly, and so on. In the course of investigation, the antitrust authorities usually collect a large amount of evidence, including market data, user feedback, complaints from competitors, etc., in order to assess whether Google's market behaviours have violated the antitrust laws.

– Google's defence

In response to antitrust investigations and lawsuits, Google typically raises the following defences:

Technological innovation and user experience: Google emphasises that its market position has been gained through technological innovation and the provision of a quality user experience. They argue that Google's search engine algorithms are constantly being optimised to more accurately understand user intent and return highly relevant search results. As a result, Google believes that its market behaviour is legitimate and beneficial.

Commercial co-operation and balancing of interests: In response to allegations of biased search results and unfair advertising promotions, Google usually argues that its search results and advertising promotion strategies are determined based on complex algorithms and bidding ranking mechanisms designed to achieve commercial co-operation and balancing of interests. Google maintains that it does not intentionally favour its own services or large customers, but strives to provide fair and objective search results for all users.

Market competition and consumer welfare: Google also emphasised the diversity of competition in the market and the enhancement of consumer welfare. They argued that despite Google's dominant position in the search engine market, there were multiple competitors and alternative products in the market for users to choose from. Therefore, Google argues that its market behaviour has not harmed market competition and consumer welfare.

– Dispute resolution and adjudication

Google has successfully defended its market position in most antitrust investigations and litigation, despite multiple questions and challenges. This is mainly due to the following factors:

Ambiguity in the application of the law: Much ambiguity and uncertainty remain in the application of antitrust law in the digital age. The antitrust authorities often face many challenges and controversies in assessing Google's market behaviour. As a result, in the absence of a clear legal basis, it is often difficult for the antitrust authorities to take severe punitive measures against Google.

Google's Market Influence: As one of the world's leading technology companies, Google has strong market influence and resources to support it. This enables Google to invest significant human, material and financial resources in its defence and response in the face of antitrust investigations and litigation.

Diversity of competition in the market: Despite Google's dominant position in the search engine market, there are multiple competitors and alternative products in the market. These competitors attract users' attention by constantly innovating and optimising their services, thus limiting Google's market behaviour to a certain extent.

[Impact and significance]

– Impact on market competition

The Google search monopoly controversy has had a far-reaching impact on market competition. On the one hand, the controversy has prompted the antitrust authorities to strengthen the regulation of the search engine market and to promote the fairness and transparency of market competition. On the other hand, the controversy has also prompted competitors to increase innovation and invest resources to improve service quality and user experience in order to gain more market share.

However, due to Google's strong position and market influence in the search engine market, competition in the market still faces many challenges and uncertainties. Competitors competing for market share often need to overcome many obstacles and difficulties in order to achieve breakthroughs and development.

– Impact on consumer rights

The Google search monopoly controversy has also had a significant impact on consumer rights. On the one hand, the controversy has prompted consumers to pay more attention to the fairness and objectivity of search results and the protection of their privacy and data security. On the other hand, the controversy has also prompted consumers to participate more actively in market competition and to monitor the market behaviour of enterprises in order to safeguard their rights and interests.

However, in practice, it is often difficult for consumers to directly assess the impartiality and objectivity of search results and the fairness of advertising and promotion. Therefore, in the absence of a clear legal basis and regulatory mechanism, the protection of consumer rights and interests still faces many challenges and uncertainties.

– Challenges and Implications for the Antitrust Laws

The Google search monopoly controversy has posed a number of challenges and lessons for antitrust law. First, the controversy has prompted the antitrust authorities to re-examine the antitrust principles and standards in the digital era in order to better respond to the new market structure and business models. Second, the controversy has also prompted antitrust authorities to strengthen cooperation and exchanges with other countries and regions in order to jointly address the market behaviour of multinational enterprises.

However, in addressing these challenges, antimonopoly authorities still face many difficulties and uncertainties. On the one hand, the ever-changing market structures and business models of the digital age pose many difficulties and challenges to the application of antitrust laws; on the other hand, the market behaviour of multinational enterprises involving multiple countries and regions requires enhanced cooperation and coordination among national antitrust authorities in order to achieve effective regulation.

[Insights and summary]

Antitrust Challenges in the Digital Era: With the rapid development and widespread application of digital technology, traditional antitrust principles and standards can no longer fully meet the needs of new market structures and business models. Therefore, antitrust authorities need to continuously innovate and improve their regulatory mechanisms to better meet the antitrust challenges of the digital era.

Regulatory challenges of multinational enterprises: Multinational enterprises have strong market influence and resources in the global market, and their market behaviours often involve multiple countries and regions, which require national antitrust authorities to strengthen cooperation and coordination in order to achieve effective regulation. However, in practice, the regulation of multinational enterprises still faces many difficulties and uncertainties, which require national antimonopoly authorities to continuously explore and improve the co-operation mechanism.

Importance of consumer rights protection: Consumer rights are the core concern of market competition and are particularly important in the digital age. Antimonopoly authorities need to strengthen the protection of consumers' rights and interests and promote fairness and transparency of market competition, while guiding enterprises to comply with laws, regulations and market rules in order to safeguard consumers' rights and interests and the public interest.

The Google Search Monopoly Dispute is an important case in the antitrust field which not only reveals the challenges and difficulties of antitrust in the digital era but also provides us with valuable experiences and insights. By analysing this case, we can better understand the applicability and limitations of the antitrust law in the digital era, as well as the complexity and importance of the regulation of multinational enterprises. At the same time, the case also encourages us to pay more attention to the importance of consumer protection, and to promote the fairness and transparency of market competition to provide a strong guarantee for the development of digital economy and platform economy. In our future antitrust work, we need to continue to explore and improve the regulatory mechanism and strengthen international cooperation and exchanges to jointly address the challenges of new market structures and business models, so as to provide strong support for the fairness of market competition and the protection of consumer rights and interests.

1.3.2 European Antitrust Practice: The Interaction of Law and Markets

[Case background]

- Qualcomm Overview

Qualcomm is the world's leading innovator of wireless technology, specialising in wireless technologies and solutions that make the world more connected. Qualcomm holds a large number of key patents in wireless communications, particularly in 3G, 4G and 5G technologies, and its patent portfolio is important to the development of the global wireless communications industry.

- Importance of Standard Essential Patents (SEPs)

Standard Essential Patents (SEPs) are patents that must be used in order to implement a technical standard. In the field of wireless communications, SEPs are crucial for device manufacturers, as they are the basis for the implementation of wireless communication functions. Due to the irreplaceable nature of SEPs, their licensing conditions directly affect the competitive situation in the market and the interests of consumers.

- Cause of the case

The European Commission has opened an antitrust investigation into Qualcomm, focusing primarily on its behaviour in relation to SEP licensing. Specifically, the investigation alleges that Qualcomm may have used its dominant market position to restrict competitors' access to the market on unfair terms. These unfair conditions may include conduct such as excessive licence fees, unreasonable licensing terms, and refusal to license.

[Processing]

- European Commission investigations

The European Commission initiated a formal investigation into Qualcomm's SEP licensing practices after receiving relevant complaints. In the course of the investigation, the Commission collected evidence from a number of sources, including market data, competitors' statements and Qualcomm's internal documents. The purpose of this evidence was to assess whether Qualcomm's behaviour in relation to SEP licensing complied with the requirements of EU antitrust law.

– Qualcomm's response

Qualcomm has adopted an aggressive defence strategy in the face of the European Commission's investigation. Qualcomm may have emphasised its contribution to innovation in wireless communications and the importance of SEP to the development of the industry. At the same time, Qualcomm may have also raised the reasonableness of its licensing strategy and denied any violation of antitrust laws.

– European Commission ruling

After in-depth investigations and analyses, the European Commission has finally found that Qualcomm has violated EU antitrust rules. The specific ruling may include the following points:

Excessive licence fees: The Commission found that the SEP licence fees charged by Qualcomm were excessive, exceeding reasonable market levels and limiting competitors' room for growth.

Unreasonable licensing terms: Qualcomm may have included some unreasonable terms in its licensing agreements, such as tying non-SEP patents and limiting the R&D capabilities of the licensee, which adversely affect competition in the market.

Licence denials: In certain circumstances, Qualcomm may deny SEP licences to certain competitors, further entrenching its market dominance.

Based on these rulings, the European Commission imposed a hefty fine on Qualcomm and required it to change its licensing strategy to ensure fair dealings with competitors.

[Impact analysis]

– Impact on Qualcomm

For Qualcomm, the European Commission's ruling is undoubtedly a major blow. The high fines have directly impacted Qualcomm's financial position and shareholders' interests. At the same time, changing its licensing strategy means that Qualcomm needs to readjust its business practices in SEP licensing to ensure compliance with antitrust laws. This may involve lowering licence fees, modifying licence terms and increasing licence transparency.

In addition, Qualcomm will need to reassess its patent licensing strategy globally to ensure that it complies with local antitrust laws and regulations in different countries and regions. This process may require Qualcomm to engage in extensive communications and consultations with competitors, regulators and industry organisations.

– Impact on competitors

For Qualcomm's competitors, the European Commission's ruling provides a more level playing field. Lower licensing fees and more reasonable licensing terms will help competitors reduce production costs and improve market competitiveness. In addition, Qualcomm's change in licensing strategy may also lead to more SEPs being licensed to competitors, further promoting technological innovation and market prosperity.

– Impact on the global communications industry

The case has had a profound impact on the global communications industry. First, it sets a new standard for SEP licensing, emphasising the principle of fair dealing between patent holders and implementers. This principle helps to maintain the order of market competition and promote technological innovation and industrial development. Secondly, the case has prompted regulators worldwide to strengthen their supervision of SEP licensing practices in order to prevent the recurrence of similar high licensing fees and unreasonable terms. Finally, the case also serves as a reminder that all companies in the industry, including patent holders and enforcers, need to comply with the requirements of the antitrust statutes in order to safeguard fair competition in the market and the interests of consumers.

[Insights and summary]

Importance of antitrust laws: Antitrust laws play an important role in maintaining the order of market competition and promoting technological innovation and industrial development. For enterprises with a dominant market position, it is important to strictly comply with the requirements of the antimonopoly law in order to prevent the abuse of market power and restriction of competition.

Fairness and reasonableness principle: In the context of Standard Essential Patent (SEP) licensing, the principle of fairness and reasonableness serves as a foundational guideline for interactions between patent holders and implementers. This principle encompasses several key aspects, including reasonable licensing fees, transparent licensing terms, and equal opportunities for obtaining licenses. Ensuring that licensing practices adhere to these standards is essential for preserving market competitiveness and fostering ongoing innovation.

Transnational regulatory cooperation: In the context of globalisation, the market behaviour of multinational enterprises often involves multiple countries and regions. Therefore, strengthening transnational regulatory cooperation is of great significance in maintaining the order of market competition. Regulators of various countries should strengthen communication and collaboration to jointly address the challenges of market behaviour of multinational enterprises.

The Qualcomm patent licensing dispute is a typical antitrust case, which reveals the fair trade issues in the SEP licensing process and the importance of antitrust law in maintaining the order of market competition. By analysing the case, we can better understand the principles and application scenarios of the antitrust law and the necessity of cross-border regulatory cooperation. At the same time, the case also provides useful reference and inspiration for the global communications industry: while promoting technological innovation and industrial development, it is important to ensure that fair competition in the market and the interests of consumers are fully protected. In the future, with the accelerated development of globalisation and digitalisation, we expect to see more regulatory cases on SEP licensing practices to further promote the healthy development of the industry and fair competition in the market.

Case 2: Facebook's Acquisition of WhatsApp
[Case background]

– Basics of Facebook and WhatsApp

Facebook is one of the world's largest social networking service companies with billions of users, providing a variety of services such as social networking, online advertising and instant messaging. WhatsApp, on the other hand, is a cross-platform instant messaging software, which has accumulated a huge user base globally with its simple interface, ad-free user experience, and powerful encrypted communication features.

– Transaction background

In 2014, Facebook announced the acquisition of WhatsApp for approximately $19 billion, a deal that attracted widespread attention in the industry.Facebook hoped that the acquisition would further consolidate its leadership in the social networking space and expand its mobile communications business by leveraging WhatsApp's dominance in the instant messaging market. However, the deal has also attracted the attention of antitrust regulators, particularly the European Commission.

– Necessity of antitrust review

The European Commission's antitrust scrutiny of Facebook's WhatsApp acquisition is based on several considerations:

Market competition impact: The European Commission is concerned that the transaction could weaken market competition in the field of instant messaging services, where Facebook and WhatsApp are among the main competitors. Once merged, the new entity may reduce competitive pressures in the market, leading to a decrease in the quality of services or an increase in prices.

Data Integration and Privacy Protection: Since both Facebook and WhatsApp have large amounts of user data, the European Commission is also concerned about the privacy protection issues that may arise from data integration. If the data of the two companies are combined and used, it may increase the risk of user privacy breaches.

Changing market dynamics: In the digital economy, market dynamics change rapidly and regulators need to ensure fair competition in the market and prevent large companies from creating market monopolies through mergers and acquisitions.

[Processing]

– Facebook's initial commitment

At the outset of the deal announcement, Facebook made a series of promises to the European Commission to allay the regulator's concerns.Facebook promised to maintain WhatsApp's independence in terms of data sharing and integration, not to force users to link WhatsApp data to their Facebook accounts, and not to use WhatsApp users' personal data to improve Facebook's ad targeting algorithms.

- European Commission investigations and assessments

Despite Facebook's initial commitment, the European Commission conducted an in-depth investigation into the transaction. In the course of the investigation, the Commission collected market data, user feedback, and expert opinions, and conducted a comprehensive assessment of the transaction's potential competitive impact on the market, data integration risks, and privacy protection issues.

- Approval with conditions

After a lengthy investigation and evaluation, the European Commission finally approved Facebook's acquisition of WhatsApp, but attached a series of strict conditions. These conditions are designed to ensure that sufficient competitive pressure remains in the market after the deal and to protect the privacy rights of users. Specific conditions may include:

Data Independence: requires Facebook to maintain the independence of WhatsApp data for a specified period of time and not to improperly integrate WhatsApp user data with data from other Facebook services.

Privacy protection: Facebook is required to comply with strict privacy protection regulations to ensure that personal data of WhatsApp users are not used for other purposes, such as ad targeting.

Market monitoring: Facebook is required to report regularly to the European Commission on the market dynamics and competition situation after the transaction, so that the regulator can keep track of the market situation and take appropriate regulatory measures.

[Impact analysis]

- The Impact on Facebook

For Facebook, the successful acquisition of WhatsApp provides a strong addition to its instant messaging services. However, the stringent conditions imposed by the European Commission have also had an impact on Facebook's business operations, and Facebook will need to invest more resources to ensure data independence and privacy protection compliance, and be subject to continuous monitoring by the regulator. In addition, Facebook will need to find effective integration strategies to realise synergies while maintaining WhatsApp's independence.

- Impact on the Instant Messaging Services Market

Despite the European Commission's approval of the deal and the conditions attached to it, the case has had an impact on the instant messaging services market. On the one hand, the success of the deal has served as a wake-up call for other instant messaging service providers to strengthen their competitiveness and seek new opportunities for growth. On the other hand, the conditions attached also ensured that sufficient competitive pressure remained in the market and prevented monopolistic behaviour by large enterprises.

– Implications for antitrust regulation

The case has important implications for antitrust regulation. First, it highlights the importance of antitrust scrutiny in the era of the digital economy. With the rapid development of the digital economy and the ever-changing market dynamics, antitrust regulators need to pay more attention to the impact on market competition and privacy protection that may be brought about by the mergers and acquisitions of large enterprises. Second, it demonstrates the antitrust regulators' determination and ability to protect market competition and consumer interests. By attaching strict conditions to the approval of transactions, the European Commission has successfully safeguarded fair competition in the market and the privacy rights of users.

[Insights and summary]

The need for antitrust review: In the era of digital economy, antitrust review is of great significance in maintaining the order of market competition and protecting consumer interests. Regulators need to strengthen their efforts to monitor the merger and acquisition behaviour of large enterprises to prevent market monopoly and unfair competition.

Antitrust law should prioritize dynamic competition and the elimination of potential competitors. Although WhatsApp had limited revenue at the time, it was growing rapidly and could have become a competitor to Facebook in the messaging space. The acquisition eliminated this potential competitive threat. Antitrust authorities must pay closer attention to 'killer acquisitions'—where dominant firms acquire emerging companies to stifle future competition. Regulation should focus more on the innovative potential of startups rather than just their current market share.

Challenges of Data Integration and Privacy Protection: With the development of big data technology and the expansion of its application, data integration and privacy protection have become important issues in antitrust reviews. Regulators need to pay attention to the possible impact of data integration on market competition and the risk of user privacy leakage, and formulate corresponding regulatory measures to prevent it.

Continuous monitoring and dynamic adjustment: Antimonopoly regulators need to continuously monitor and dynamically adjust merger and acquisition behaviour in the market. By regularly assessing the post-transaction market dynamics and competition situation and adjusting regulatory measures, they ensure fair competition in the market and that consumer interests are adequately safeguarded.

The case of Facebook's acquisition of WhatsApp is a typical case of antitrust review in the digital economy era. The analysis of this case shows the importance of antitrust review in maintaining the order of market competition and protecting consumer interests, as well as the challenges and difficulties it faces. In the future, with the rapid development of the digital economy and changing market dynamics, antitrust regulators will need to pay more attention to the mergers and acquisitions of large corporations and formulate corresponding regulatory measures to ensure fair competition in the market and fully protect the interests of consumers. At the same time, we also need to recognise that in the era of digital economy, antitrust review needs to be constantly innovated and improved to adapt to the new market environment and regulatory needs.

1.3.3 Antitrust Practice in Asia: Challenges and Responses

Case 1: China's Alibaba Monopoly Investigation
[Case background]

– Alibaba Group Overview

Alibaba Group is China's leading e-commerce company with a number of well-known business segments such as Taobao, Tmall, Aliyun and Alipay. As a leader in China's e-commerce market, Alibaba has not only driven the development of China's e-commerce industry, but has also made a wide impact on a global scale.

– Overview of "pick one from two" behaviour

"Either/or" behaviour, which usually refers to large e-commerce platforms taking advantage of their dominant position in the market to exclude or restrict competitors by requiring merchants to exclusively sell their goods or services on their platforms [8]. The case of Alibaba is a case in point. In Alibaba's case, the "choose one" behaviour is mainly reflected in its requirement for merchants to choose between Tmall and other e-commerce platforms (e.g., Jingdong, Pinduoduo, etc.), forcing the merchants to sell their goods only on the Tmall platform.

– Background of the antitrust investigation

With the rapid development of China's Internet platform economy, market competition has become increasingly fierce. However, some large platform companies have gradually surfaced to take advantage of their market position to engage in unfair competition. In order to protect fair competition and consumer interests, the State Administration of Market Supervision and Administration of the People's Republic of China (AMSA) has decided to conduct an anti-monopoly investigation into Alibaba Group, focusing on whether its "two-for-one" behaviour constitutes an abuse of its dominant market position.

[Processing]

– Investigation launched

In 2020, China's State Administration for Market Supervision and Administration formally launched an anti-monopoly investigation into Alibaba Group. At the initial stage of the investigation, the regulator collected a large amount of market data, feedback from merchants and expert opinions, and conducted a comprehensive assessment of Alibaba's market position in the e-commerce platform sector, the implementation of its "two-for-one" behaviour and its impact on market competition.

– Evidence collection and analysis

In the course of the investigation, the regulator collected a wide range of evidence relevant to the case through a variety of means, such as reviewing company documents, interviewing relevant personnel and collecting testimonies from merchants. The evidence included not only Alibaba's internal documents and marketing strategies, but also complaints and feedback from merchants and industry reports. By analysing this evidence, the regulator gradually clarified the details of Alibaba's "two choices" and its impact on the market [1]. The regulator has gradually clarified the details of Alibaba's "choose one" behaviour and its impact on the market [1].

– Application and assessment of the law

In the course of the investigation, the regulator also conducted an in-depth study of the relevant laws and regulations, in particular the provisions of the Anti-Monopoly Law of the People's Republic of China on the abuse of dominant market position. By analysing Alibaba's market conduct in comparison with the legal provisions, the regulator assessed the legality and compliance of its conduct, which provided a legal basis for the subsequent treatment decision.

– Progress in processing and outcome expectations

To date, on 10 April 2021, the General Administration of Market Supervision (GAMS) issued a final penalty decision against Alibaba Group for its "choose-one-or-two" monopoly in the market for online retail platform services in China. After a detailed investigation, it was found that Alibaba had abused its dominant market position since 2015 by mandating that merchants on its platforms could only choose to sell on its platforms and could not set up shop or participate in promotional activities on other competing platforms. This behaviour restricted market competition and damaged the legitimate rights and interests of merchants and consumers.

As punishment, the General Administration of Market Supervision (GAMS) ordered Alibaba to cease its illegal behaviour and imposed a fine of 4% of its 2019 sales in China (i.e., 18.228 billion yuan), in accordance with the Anti-Monopoly Law. The penalty is an important sign of antitrust enforcement in China's platform economy. In addition, the regulator issued an Administrative Guidance Letter to Alibaba, requiring it to make comprehensive corrections and submit self-inspection compliance reports for three consecutive years.

[Impact analysis]

– Impact on Alibaba

For Alibaba, the antitrust investigation will undoubtedly have some impact on its business operations and market reputation. If it is ultimately found to have abused its dominant market position, Alibaba may be required to pay hefty fines and adjust its marketing strategy. In addition, the investigation process itself will also have some impact on Alibaba's brand image and merchant relations. However, in the long run, strict antitrust regulation will help Alibaba to regulate its own behaviour, improve its competitiveness in the market and win the trust of more merchants and consumers.

– Impact on the e-commerce platform industry

The Alibaba monopoly investigation will not only have an impact on Alibaba itself, but will also have a far-reaching impact on the entire e-commerce platform industry. On the one hand, the investigation will prompt other e-commerce platforms to strengthen their self-discipline and awareness of compliance, and to avoid committing similar acts of unfair competition. On the other hand, the investigation will also promote the development of the entire industry in a healthier and more orderly direction, creating a fairer and more transparent market environment for merchants and consumers.

– Impact on the Chinese economy and global markets

As one of the leading companies in China's e-commerce industry, Alibaba's antitrust investigation will not only concern the healthy development of China's economy, but will also have certain impact on the global market. On the one hand, the investigation will provide important cases and reference experience for the Chinese government to strengthen the antitrust regulation of the Internet platform economy; on the other hand, the investigation will also prompt the global Internet giants to re-examine their code of conduct and compliance requirements in the Chinese market, and to avoid the regulatory risks arising from inappropriate competitive behaviours.

[Insights and summary]

The Need for Antitrust Regulation: In the era of the digital economy, the rapid rise of internet platform-based enterprises has emerged as a major driver of global economic growth. However, as these platforms consolidate their market positions and expand their influence, concerns over potential unfair competitive practices have become increasingly prominent. Strengthening antitrust regulation is therefore essential to safeguarding fair market competition and ensuring the healthy and orderly development of the platform economy. The Alibaba "pick one from two" case demonstrates that the healthy development of the platform economy must be premised on fair competition. Antitrust enforcement does not negate a company's market success but aims to prevent the abuse of dominant positions that distorts competition. In the future, as the digital economy grows more complex, antitrust regulation will place greater emphasis on combining technological means with legal frameworks. Platform enterprises must strike a balance between innovation and compliance.

Flexibility in the application of laws: In antitrust investigations, how to accurately apply relevant laws and regulations is a key issue. Due to the specificity and complexity of the Internet platform economy, it may be difficult for the traditional antitrust legal framework to fully adapt to the regulatory needs in the new situation. Therefore, regulators need to maintain a certain degree of flexibility on the basis of following the basic legal principles and formulate targeted regulatory measures according to the specific situation.

The antitrust investigation into Alibaba represents one of China's significant initiatives to strengthen regulatory oversight of monopolistic practices within the platform-based digital economy. A thorough analysis of this case highlights the critical role antitrust regulation plays in safeguarding fair market competition, while also revealing the challenges and complexities inherent in enforcing such regulations. As the digital economy continues to evolve and market competition intensifies, antitrust enforcement is expected to become increasingly vital and intricate. This calls for continuous refinement of legal frameworks and regulatory mechanisms, along with enhanced international cooperation and dialogue, to support the development of a more effective global antitrust governance system. At the same time, it is important to recognize that antitrust regulation is not a one-time endeavor; rather, it is a long-term commitment that requires coordinated efforts from governments, enterprises, and consumers alike.

Case 2: Kakao Talk Antitrust Controversy in South Korea
[Case background]

– Kakao Talk Overview

Kakao Talk is one of the most popular instant messaging apps in Korea, providing not only basic chatting functions, but also integrating a variety of life services, such as payment, games, shopping, etc., which has become an indispensable part of Koreans' daily lives. With its large user base and highly integrated service ecosystem, Kakao Talk occupies a pivotal position in the Korean market.

– The formation of a dominant market position

With its advanced technology, rich features and good user experience, Kakao Talk has stood out in the highly competitive instant messaging market and gradually established its dominant position in the Korean market. Kakao Talk's influence is growing with the increasing number of users and market share.

– Allegations of data monopoly and unfair business practices

As Kakao Talk's market position has consolidated, allegations of its use of data to monopolise and unfair business practices have grown. Specific allegations include:

Data monopoly: By collecting and analysing user data, Kakao Talk has acquired a wealth of valuable information on user behaviour, preferences and needs. However, some competitors and third-party service providers have accused Kakao Talk of using its data dominance to restrict competition by preventing other platforms from accessing key data, thereby maintaining its market monopoly.

Unfair pricing: Some critics argue that Kakao Talk's pricing strategy for certain services is unfair. Due to its dominant market position, there is a possibility that Kakao Talk may adopt discriminatory pricing strategies by setting higher thresholds or charging higher fees to its competitors so as to further consolidate its market position.

– Necessity of antitrust regulation

In the face of Kakao Talk's dominant market position and the controversy it has generated, the Korean government has realised the importance of strengthening antitrust regulation. In order to protect fair competition in the market, safeguard consumers' rights and promote the healthy development of the Internet industry, the Korea Fair Trade Commission (KFTC) has initiated a number of antitrust investigations against Kakao Talk.

[Processing]

– Initiation of antitrust investigations

The Korea Fair Trade Commission (KFTC) decided to launch an antitrust investigation into Kakao Talk after receiving relevant complaints and reports. At the initial stage of the investigation, the KFTC focused on Kakao Talk's market share, user base, service ecosystem, and pricing strategy in the instant messaging market.

– Evidence collection and review

In the course of the investigation, the KFTC collected evidence extensively through a variety of means, including reviewing company documents, interviewing relevant personnel, and collecting user feedback and third-party data. Such evidence included Kakao Talk's internal documents, market reports, user data, and competitors' complaint materials. Through careful examination and analysis of this evidence, the KFTC gradually grasped Kakao Talk's market behaviour and its impact on market competition.

– Points of contention and findings

During the course of the investigation, the dispute centred on the following areas:

Data Monopoly Issues: The KFTC conducted an in-depth investigation into Kakao Talk's data collection and use practices. Although Kakao Talk denied using its data dominance to restrict competition, the KFTC found that it did have data sharing and access restrictions in some instances. These restrictions may have affected the business development of competitors and third-party service providers.

Unfair Pricing Issues: The KFTC conducted a detailed review of Kakao Talk's pricing strategy. Although Kakao Talk claimed that its pricing was reasonable and transparent, the KFTC found that its pricing did discriminate on certain services. For example, by setting higher access fees or providing poorer quality of service to competitors.

– Handling measures and rectification requirements

Based on the results of the investigation and the provisions of relevant laws and regulations, the KFTC has put forward a series of corrective requirements and recommended measures for Kakao Talk. These measures include:

Open Data Interfaces: Kakao Talk is required to open its data interfaces and platform resources to allow competitors and third-party service providers fairer access to and use of relevant data.

Adjustment of pricing strategy: Kakao Talk was asked to adjust its pricing strategy to ensure that all users and service providers are treated equally and that discriminatory pricing practices are avoided.

Strengthening compliance management: Kakao Talk was required to strengthen its internal compliance management, establish a comprehensive antitrust compliance system, and ensure that its market behaviour meets the requirements of relevant laws and regulations.

- Follow-up and monitoring

In order to ensure that Kakao Talk is able to effectively fulfil the rectification requirements and continuously comply with relevant laws and regulations, the KFTC will continue to follow up and monitor its market conduct. At the same time, the KFTC will also strengthen cooperation and communication with other regulatory agencies to jointly promote the healthy development of the Internet industry in Korea.

[Impact analysis]

- Impact on Kakao Talk

For Kakao Talk, the antitrust investigation and measures will undoubtedly have an impact on its business operations and market reputation. On the one hand, the opening up of data interfaces and the adjustment of pricing strategies may increase its operating costs and affect its profitability; on the other hand, the strict antitrust regulation will also force it to strengthen its internal compliance management and regulate its market behaviours. However, in the long run, these measures will help Kakao Talk to enhance its competitiveness in the market and win the trust and support of more users and merchants.

- Impact on the Korean Internet industry

The antitrust investigation not only targeted Kakao Talk individually but also had a far-reaching impact on the Korean Internet industry as a whole. On the one hand, it has prompted other Internet platforms to strengthen their self-discipline and awareness of compliance to avoid similar unfair competition; on the other hand, it has pushed the Korean government to strengthen the antitrust supervision of Internet platforms and improve the relevant laws and regulations to provide a strong guarantee for the healthy development of the industry.

- Impact on other countries in Asia

As a representative case in Asia, the Kakao Talk antitrust dispute in South Korea provides valuable experience and lessons for other countries. On the one hand, it demonstrates the important role of antitrust regulation in maintaining fair competition in the market and protecting consumers' rights and interests; on the other hand, it reminds other countries that they must pay attention to the importance of antitrust regulation while promoting the development of the Internet industry and take effective measures to deal with it.

[Insights and summary]

Importance of antitrust regulation: In the era of digital economy, the market influence of Internet platform enterprises is increasing and their possible unfair competition behaviours are becoming more and more prominent. Therefore, strengthening anti-monopoly regulation is of great significance in maintaining fair competition in the market and protecting consumers' rights and interests.

Balance between data protection and sharing: The balance between data protection and sharing is a key issue in antitrust investigations. On the one hand, user privacy and data security must be protected; on the other hand, it is also important to ensure the reasonable flow and sharing of data to promote market competition and innovation.

Improvement of Laws and Policies: In the face of the specificity and complexity of the Internet platform economy, the traditional antitrust law and policy system may be difficult to fully adapt to the regulatory needs under the new situation. Therefore, it is necessary to continuously improve relevant laws, regulations and policy measures to meet the development needs of the digital economy era.

The Kakao Talk antitrust controversy in South Korea is one of the important cases in which the Korean government has strengthened antitrust regulation of Internet platforms. By analysing the case in detail, we can see the important role of antitrust regulation in maintaining fair competition in the market and protecting consumers' rights and interests, as well as the challenges and difficulties it faces. In the future, as the digital economy continues to develop and market competition becomes more intense, antitrust regulation will become even more important and complex.

1.4 Antitrust Challenges and Trends in the Digital Economy

1.4.1 Emerging Markets and Technologies Challenging Traditional Antitrust Laws

In today's fast-developing digital economy, the rise of emerging markets and technologies has not only changed the mode of operation of traditional industries, but also posed a serious challenge to the theoretical basis and implementation of antitrust law. In particular, the popularity of technologies such as big data, artificial intelligence, and cloud computing has enabled companies to build strong market barriers through data dominance and technological innovation, and thus form a monopoly position. The following will discuss in detail how data-driven monopolies, bilateral markets under the platform economy, and cross-border integration and ecological competition pose challenges to antitrust law and propose corresponding strategies to deal with them.

The Challenge of Data-Driven Monopolies

– Data as a new factor of production

With the rapid advancement of information technology, data has emerged as a new factor of production in the digital economy era. By collecting, analyzing, and leveraging vast amounts of user data, companies can gain more precise insights into market demands, optimize product design, and enhance service experiences. However, once data accumulates beyond a certain scale, it transforms into a strategic asset that enables firms to establish significant market barriers. Large technology companies, by virtue of their massive user bases, are able to continuously harvest and analyze behavioral data, thereby gaining a competitive edge that is often insurmountable. This advantage extends beyond personalized products and services, encompassing areas such as market forecasting, pricing strategies, and targeted marketing, thus raising profound concerns about the potential for entrenched dominance and diminished market contestability [9].

– Mechanisms of data monopoly formation

The formation of a data monopoly is a complex and subtle process. First, enterprises attract a large number of users by providing free services and innovate their business models through the data generated by those users. As the scale of users and the amount of data increase, companies are able to continuously optimise their products and services to further consolidate their market position [1] Secondly, enterprises can limit the number of users through technological means. Second, enterprises restrict competitors' ability to access user data through technical means, such as setting up technical barriers and adopting exclusivity agreements, so as to maintain their data monopoly. Finally, enterprises use the results of data analysis to guide strategic decision-making and achieve optimal allocation and efficient use of market resources.

– Adaptation challenges in antitrust law

Traditional antitrust laws focus on traditional market factors such as market share, market access barriers, and pricing strategies, while the identification and assessment of data-driven monopolies is out of reach. On the one hand, the hidden and complex nature of data monopolies makes it difficult for regulators to accurately judge the market power of companies; on the other hand, the dynamic and changing nature of data monopolies makes it difficult to effectively implement antitrust measures. Therefore, antitrust law needs to adapt to the development needs of the digital economy era and introduce new analytical frameworks and assessment standards to meet the challenges of data-driven monopoly [3] The following is a summary of the findings of the study.

1.4.2 Bilateral Markets in the Platform Economy and Emerging Issues in Antitrust

– Characteristics of bilateral markets

The core feature of the platform economy, as one of the important forms in the era of the digital economy, lies in the construction of a trading platform that connects bilateral or multilateral users. On this platform, interactions and transactions between users become the main source of value creation. However, the characteristics of bilateral markets also make the analysis of market competition more complicated. Firstly, there are network effects and lock-in effects in bilateral markets, i.e., an increase in the number of users attracts more users to join the platform, thus creating a positive feedback loop; at the same time, the transaction data and credit history accumulated by users on the platform also increase their transfer costs. Secondly, the pricing strategy of bilateral markets is also different from that of traditional markets, in which platforms often adopt free or even subsidised strategies for users on one side to attract them to join the platform, and profit from advertisements and value-added services for users on the other side [10]. The platforms are also different from traditional marketplaces in terms of pricing.

– Market forces assessment challenges

Assessing the market power of an enterprise under bilateral market conditions has become a major challenge for antitrust law. Traditional market share indicators may be ineffective in bilateral markets because market share does not fully reflect the true position and influence of an enterprise in the market. For example, in some platforms, even if a firm has a high market share, it may not be able to effectively restrict the entry of competitors due to network and lock-in effects. Therefore, antitrust authorities need to introduce new analytical tools and methods to assess the market power of firms in bilateral markets, such as price elasticity analysis and assessment of cross-network effects.

– Antimonopoly policy reorientation

Antimonopoly policies need to be adjusted accordingly to the characteristics of the bilateral market. On the one hand, it is necessary to strengthen the regulation of the data collection and use behaviour of platform enterprises to prevent them from taking advantage of data to engage in unfair competition; on the other hand, it is necessary to optimize the market access and exit mechanism to reduce the transfer cost of users and promote market competition; and at the same time, it is also necessary to improve the anti-monopoly legal system to clarify the rights and obligations of the platform enterprises and regulate their market behaviours.

1.4.3 Cross-Border Integration and Ecological Competition: The New Antitrust Landscape

– Blurring of industry boundaries

In the era of digital economy, industry boundaries are becoming increasingly blurred and cross-border integration has become the norm. Enterprises continue to expand their business scope and market areas through technological innovation and business model innovation to form a pattern of diversified development. This cross-border integration not only breaks the competition pattern of traditional industries, but also gives rise to new business models and market ecology. For example, through big data and artificial intelligence technology, Internet enterprises have entered various fields such as finance, healthcare and education, forming a cross-industry competitive advantage.

– New pattern of ecological competition

Cross-border integration promotes eco-competition among enterprises, i.e., competition among enterprises is no longer limited to a single product or service, but extends to the entire ecosystem. In this ecosystem, enterprises attract a large number of users and partners by building open platforms and rich application scenarios to form mutually beneficial and win-win cooperative relationships. However, this kind of eco-competition also brings new problems and challenges, such as the closed nature of the ecosystem, exclusivity, and the squeeze on small businesses and entrepreneurs.

1.5 Antitrust Strategies for Meeting the Challenges of the Digital Economy

In the digital economy, antitrust faces unprecedented challenges. This is not only because of the rapid changes in market structures and business models, but also because of the key role of data, algorithms and technology platforms in competition. Therefore, antitrust strategies must address these complex issues in an integrated manner from the perspective of improving the legal system, strengthening international and cross-sectoral cooperation, and interdisciplinary integration.

1.5.1 The Path to Improvement of a Modernised Antimonopoly Legal Framework

In the context of the digital economy, the existing anti-monopoly legal framework shows certain limitations. The traditional legal system was mainly designed for the industrial economic era, while the digital economy has brought new forms of monopoly, such as data monopoly and platform monopoly. For this reason, the antitrust legal system needs to be improved in the following aspects:

Clarifying the legal definition of data monopoly and regulatory measures: As data has become an important asset for the core competitiveness of enterprises, how to define data monopoly and effectively regulate it has become a new topic for antitrust law. The legal system needs to clarify the ownership and use of data and its role in the market, and formulate targeted legal provisions and penalties.

Introducing dynamic market assessment tools: Existing market assessment methods (e.g. market share analyses) are too static when dealing with dynamic and complex digital markets. By introducing tools such as network effect analysis and algorithmic transparency assessment, the influence and monopoly potential of companies in the digital market can be more accurately assessed [11]. The following are some examples of such tools.

Enhanced regulation of cross-platform and ecosystem monopolies: Large technology companies often strengthen their market control by integrating across platforms and establishing closed ecosystems. Antitrust laws need to establish special regulatory rules for such behaviour to prevent firms from abusing their dominant market position to unfairly compete or exclude other market participants [12]. The antitrust laws need to establish special rules to prevent companies from abusing their dominant position to compete or exclude other market participants [12].

1.5.2 Enhancing International and Cross-Sectoral Collaboration: Tackling the Monopoly of Globalisation

The digital economy is global and cross-border in nature, and monopolistic behaviour often involves multiple countries and different areas of regulation. For this reason, strengthening international cooperation and cross-sectoral collaboration is key to addressing monopolistic behaviour in the digital economy:

Promoting global antitrust regulatory harmonisation: Countries should try to harmonise their enforcement of antitrust laws to prevent regulatory arbitrage by multinational enterprises taking advantage of differences in different legal systems. By establishing an international antitrust cooperation mechanism, it is possible to share investigation results, coordinate enforcement actions, and develop globally uniform rules for competition in the digital economy [5].

Cross-sectoral joint enforcement: Monopolistic behaviour in the digital economy often involves multiple regulatory areas, such as data protection, cybersecurity and consumer protection. Therefore, there is a need to establish a cross-sectoral joint enforcement mechanism to coordinate the actions of various regulatory agencies and create synergies. For example, antitrust agencies could work with data protection and information security agencies to jointly monitor the compliance of large technology companies with regard to data use and market behaviour.

Strengthening regional cooperation: At the regional level, in economies such as the EU, antitrust regulations are already promoting harmonisation and coordination within the region. By strengthening regional cooperation, member States can share resources and act in concert in antitrust enforcement and effectively respond to the monopolistic behaviour of multinational enterprises in regional markets.

1.5.3 The Rise of Computational Antitrust: Technology-Driven Legal Innovation

The complexity of the digital economy requires that antitrust strategies not only rely on law and economics, but also incorporate interdisciplinary disciplines such as computer science and data science, which has given rise to the new field of "computational antitrust" [13] [13]. This has given rise to the new field of "computational antitrust" [13]:

Application of Big Data and Artificial Intelligence: Antitrust regulation can analyse market behaviour and corporate competitive strategies through big data technology, and use artificial intelligence algorithms to make market predictions and identify monopolistic behaviour. Computational antitrust achieves real-time monitoring of the market through technological means, and improves the accuracy and responsiveness of antitrust enforcement [14].

Algorithm Transparency and Fairness Assessment: In the digital economy, firms often use complex algorithms to conduct market operations, such as price discrimination and market segmentation. By introducing algorithmic review and transparency assessment mechanisms, antitrust authorities can better understand and regulate these algorithms to prevent them from being misused to harm market competition.

Building a digital toolbox for antitrust: Developing specialised antitrust tools and platforms to help enforcement officers conduct competition analysis in complex market environments. These tools can integrate market data, laws and regulations, and algorithmic models to provide all-round technical support for antitrust investigations. The tools can integrate market data, laws and regulations, and algorithmic models to provide comprehensive technical support for antitrust investigations [15, 16].

Through the above strategies, antitrust regulation can more effectively adapt to the complexity of the digital economy, maintain fair competition in the market, and promote innovation and the protection of consumer rights.

1.6 Summary of the Chapter

This chapter presents a comprehensive examination of the origins of antitrust law, the evolution of major antitrust regimes across key countries and regions, and the emerging challenges and policy responses in the context of the modern digital economy. As a core legal instrument for safeguarding market competition, antitrust law has undergone continuous development since the late nineteenth century, shaped by the transformations brought about by the Industrial Revolution. Over time, diverse legislative and enforcement practices have emerged globally, reflecting the varying economic conditions and market dynamics faced by different jurisdictions. These distinct historical and institutional contexts have given rise to a range of antitrust legal systems, each tailored to address specific national or regional needs.

In global antitrust practice, case studies from representative countries in the United States, Europe and Asia demonstrate the importance and complexity of antitrust law in maintaining fair competition in the marketplace and curbing unfair competition. Especially in the era of digital economy, with the rapid development of emerging technologies and market models, antitrust law faces unprecedented challenges. Data monopoly, bilateral market characteristics in the platform economy, and ecological competition in cross-border integration have all posed a severe test to traditional antitrust theory and legal framework.

To address these challenges, this chapter suggests strategies ranging from improving the antitrust legal system, strengthening international and cross-sectoral cooperation, and introducing interdisciplinary computational antitrust. These strategies not only emphasise the modernisation and flexibility of the legal framework, but also highlight the important role of technological tools in antitrust regulation. Through these measures, the antitrust law will be able to respond more effectively to the complexity of the digital economy, safeguard fair competition in the marketplace.

References

1. ZHANG Rong-gang,WEI Chuan (2023) Strategies for enhancing the effectiveness of anti-monopoly LegaRegulation in the platform Area 54(06):60–71.DOI:https://doi.org/10.13764/j.cnki.ncds.2023.06.004
2. Lan Qingxin Shi Fangyuan (2022) Monopoly Problems and Countermeasures for The Development of Internet Platform in China2022(04):80–88.DOI:https://doi.org/10.14110/j.cnki.cn-37-1059/d.2022.04.017
3. JANYE YAN, YUE ZHANG(2024) Antitrust regulation in the digital platform economy:status, Challengesand prospects, College of Economics and Management.2024,(02):92-106. DOI:https://doi.org/10.19313/j.cnki.cn10-1223/f.20240312.003
4. Wang X-y (2018) The Implementation of China's Anti-Monopoly Law for 10Years:Achievements and Challenges. 2018(05):128–137

5. JN Meirong, DONG Yilin (2022) Conflict of Extraterritorial Merger Remedies and International Cooperation Mechanism. 2022(02):133–149+195. https://doi.org/10.16094/j.cnki.1005-0221.2022.02.004
6. GILBERT R J, MELAMED A D. ANTITRUST FOR INNOVATION: A PROGRESS REPORT[J]. GW Competition & Innovation Lab Working Paper Series, 2024 (2024/9)
7. CHEN Bing,FU Xiao-ou (2024) Re-exploration of Requlatory Methods for Self-preferential Behaviour of Platform-between Commercial Competition and Competition Compliance2024,(02):52–61
8. Lin, Shao (2022). The logic and development of anti-monopoly law regulation of E-commerce platform's "choose one" behaviour. Shanghai Legal Studies,2022,7(01):490–506
9. Funta R, Buttler D (2023) The digital economy and legal challenges[J]. InterEULawEast: Journal for the international and european law, economics and market integrations 10(1):145–160
10. Wang C., Chen H., Yang Y. Research on monopoly issues and regulatory suggestions of platform economy in the digital economy era. Electron Gov, 2021,(05):2–11.DOI:https://doi.org/10.16582/j.cnki.dzzw.2021.05.001
11. Lamao S (2025) Legal regulation of data monopoly on internet platforms in China. J Comput Electron Inf Manag 17(1):38–45
12. ZHENG Pengcheng, LONG Sen (2022). The regulatory logic and path of "big data Price discrimination" by platforms from the perspective of publicity. Journal of Jishou University(Social Sciences Edition), 2022, 43(6): 29–40
13. XIONG Hong-ru. Platform monopoly in the development of digital economy in China andts governance strategies Reform, 2019, (07): 52–61
14. Wu L (2023) Research on anti-monopoly regulations against algorithmic Price discrimination. Journal of Education, Humanities and Social Sciences 14:157–165
15. Gillis TB, Spiess JL (2019) Big data and discrimination. Univ Chic Law Rev 86(2):459–488
16. Cui R, Li J, Li M et al (2021) Wholesale price discrimination in global sourcing. Manuf Serv Oper Manag 23(5):1096–1117

Chapter 2
Antitrust in the Digital Economy

Abstract This chapter traces the evolution of the digital economy from early conceptions of ICT-enabled commerce to today's data-driven, platform-centred ecosystems. We first clarify narrow and broad definitions adopted by international bodies and policy communities, then show how pervasive digitization has reshaped market structure and conduct. Multi-sided platforms lower entry barriers while amplifying network effects, often yielding oligopolistic dynamics and "winner-takes-all" outcomes. Data—characterized by high fixed and near-zero marginal costs, scalability, and spillovers—has emerged as a core competitive asset, enabling precision matching, rapid product iteration, and, in some cases, new levers of market power.

We catalogue salient unfair practices observed in platform markets, including exclusivity arrangements, self-preferencing, data blocking, personalized (discriminatory) pricing, tying/bundling, strategic exploitation of network effects, and algorithmically facilitated coordination. These behaviors are frequently opaque and adaptive, complicating detection, proof, and timely remedies. We argue that traditional antitrust—anchored in price-centric market definition, static indicators of dominance, and ex-post casework—faces material limits when applied to zero-price services, cross-market leverage, and black-box algorithms.

In response, jurisdictions have begun to modernize their toolkits. The EU has introduced ex-ante obligations for "gatekeepers" alongside horizontal platform governance rules; Germany has updated abuse control for firms of paramount cross market significance; the United States has refreshed merger guidance for digital markets; Japan has advanced transparency requirements for mobile ecosystems; and China has revised competition and data-governance statutes to address algorithmic and data-based abuses. We conclude by motivating a complementary "computational antitrust" agenda—combining procedural due process and rule-of-reason analysis with model-based screening, simulation, and audit of data and algorithms—to better balance innovation and fairness in the digital economy.

Keywords Digital economy · Platform economy · Multi-sided markets · Data as a production factor · Network effects · Data monopoly · Algorithmic collusion · Price discrimination · Self preferencing and exclusivity · Antitrust enforcement · Ex-ante digital regulation · Computational antitrust

W. Liu, *Computational Antitrust*, Artificial Intelligence and the Rule of Law,
https://doi.org/10.1007/978-981-95-5037-1_2

2.1 History of the Digital Economy

2.1.1 Overview of the Digital Economy

The concept of the digital economy was first introduced in 1996 by Don Tapscott in his influential work *Digital Economy: Opportunities and Challenges in the Age of Network Intelligence*. Through a series of case studies, Tapscott illustrated how the widespread adoption of information technology was fundamentally transforming societal modes of production and daily life. He defined the digital economy as an economic system that extensively leverages information and communication technologies (ICT), encompassing e-commerce and other emerging business models. Building on this foundation, Lamb (1999) further conceptualized the digital economy as the use of digital technologies in the production and delivery of goods and services.

Miller and Wilsdon (2001) further pointed out that the digital economy, as a revolution on the Internet, not only changes the paradigm of economic and social development and gradually become a new impetus for scientific and technological innovation, but also provides a new way to promote the development of the digital economy. Miller and Wilsdon (2001) further state that the digital economy, as an Internet revolution, has not only changed the paradigm of economic and social development and gradually become the new driving force of scientific and technological innovation, but also provides a way to use digital technology to achieve sustainable development of human society.

With the rapid advancement of the internet and digital technologies, the connotation of the digital economy has significantly expanded. Leading international research institutions and domestic scholars have systematically defined the digital economy from various perspectives. In a narrow sense, the digital economy is considered an industrial economy. For instance, France's Digital Economy Monitoring Center characterizes it as a set of industries that rely heavily on information and communication technologies (ICT), encompassing sectors such as telecommunications and the internet industry [1].

From a broader perspective, the digital economy refers to a wide range of economic activities. Notable definitions include those provided by the *G20 Digital Economy Development and Cooperation Initiative*, the White Paper on China's Digital Economy Development issued by the China Academy of Information and Communications Technology (CAICT), and the International Monetary Fund (IMF) [2].

First, the *G20 Initiative*, which has been widely recognized in China, defines the digital economy as "a series of economic activities that use digitized knowledge and information as key production factors, modern information networks as critical carriers, and the effective application of ICT as an important driver for improving efficiency and optimizing economic structures."

Second, the *White Paper on China's Digital Economy Development* builds upon this definition by emphasizing digital technological innovation as a core driving force. It advocates for deep integration of digital technologies with traditional industries and the real economy, thereby promoting economic transformation and enabling a reconfiguration of governance paradigms.

Third, the IMF delineates both narrow and broad interpretations of the digital economy. The narrow definition refers primarily to online platform-based activities, such as those found in platform and sharing economies. The broader definition encompasses all economic activities involving digitization. This dual-framework has gained wide international recognition and has been frequently adopted in academic and policy-oriented studies.

Today, as digital technologies increasingly permeate everyday life, the digital economy is reaching a stage of maturity. New technological revolutions are giving rise to innovative economic models, where digital and physical economies are deeply intertwined. This fusion is driving the emergence of sectors such as e-commerce, social media, and instant messaging, and enabling the development of cutting-edge technologies including artificial intelligence, big data, and cloud computing. As a result, the digital economy is becoming a key engine for global economic growth. At the same time, it poses new challenges—ranging from data privacy and cybersecurity to shifts in market competition structures.

2.1.2 History of the Digital Economy

In recent years, under the extensive impetus of the scientific and technological revolution, emerging technologies such as big data, artificial intelligence, cloud computing, blockchain and so on have emerged, which have brought great changes to the daily lives of human beings and at the same time brought new opportunities for social and industrial development. Against the backdrop of the global economic slowdown and sluggish recovery, the digital economy has accelerated under the impetus of digital technology and has become an important driving force for the recovery of the national economy of various countries. China's digital economy has been developing rapidly in recent years, and from 2017 to 2022, the scale of China's digital economy development has been expanding, with the output value steadily growing from RMB 27.2 trillion in 2017 to RMB 50.2 trillion in 2022, and the proportion of the digital economy in the GDP has also been gradually increasing, having risen from 32.9% to 41.5% in 2017, and the digital economy has become an indispensable factor in driving the indispensable factor in China's economic recovery. Meanwhile, the 2022 Digital China Development Report shows that China's digital economy grew by 10.3% year-on-year in nominal terms in that year, and the scale of the digital industry grew steadily, with data production reaching 8.1ZB, up 22.7% year-on-year, and the global share reaching 10.5%, ranking second in the world.

China is accelerating the construction of the data factor market by promoting technological innovations such as 5G and artificial intelligence, improving the industrial system of the digital economy, enhancing the total factor productivity of the digital economy, and supporting the accumulation and growth of new quality productivity. The report of the 20th Party Congress pointed out that it is necessary to accelerate the development of the digital economy, promote the deep integration of the digital economy and the real economy, and create internationally competitive digital industry clusters.2024 The meeting of the regular session of the National People's Congress in July pointed out that it is necessary to understand and promote the high-quality development of the digital economy from the height of the overall situation, to promote the deep integration of digital technology and the real economy, and to promote the industrialisation of digital industry and the digitalisation of industry, so as to comprehensively empower the development of the economy and society; It is necessary to adhere to reform, innovation and open cooperation, continuously optimise the environment for the development of the digital economy, collaborate to improve the data base system and digital infrastructure, and promote the market allocation of data elements; it is necessary to enhance the innovation capacity of platform enterprises, and promote the sustained and healthy development of the platform economy.

In the era of the digital economy, traditional market actors—such as brick-and-mortar stores and intermediaries—have gradually been displaced or had their roles transformed by emerging e-commerce platforms. These platforms have become new market participants, leveraging digital technologies and online infrastructures to directly connect producers with consumers, thereby reshaping market structures. By lowering entry barriers through digitization, e-commerce platforms have enabled small businesses and individual entrepreneurs to participate more easily in market competition, intensifying overall market dynamics.

The rise of e-commerce has disrupted the monopoly positions traditionally held by legacy industries, leading to more diverse and intensified forms of competition. Consumers now enjoy greater freedom of choice, while firms engage in increasingly fierce rivalries to secure market share. Against the backdrop of digital transformation, e-commerce platforms harness big data analytics and personalized recommendation algorithms to better anticipate consumer needs, offering higher-quality products and services that grant them a competitive edge. Meanwhile, conventional modes of market operation face mounting challenges from these digital innovations, as e-commerce introduces greater transparency, efficiency, and intelligence into market mechanisms, thereby enhancing the speed and performance of market operations.

Furthermore, the growth of e-commerce has catalyzed the emergence of novel business models and operational paradigms—such as the sharing economy and social commerce—that have fundamentally altered the rules and modes of market transactions. These changes have had a profound impact on competitive dynamics, reshaping both the structure and outcomes of market competition.

2.2 Impact of Digitisation on Competition in the Market

2.2.1 Digital Economy Platforms as New Market Players

Digital economy platforms, through the comprehensive capabilities of data and algorithms, have broken the traditional time and space constraints, linked various types of subjects, provided comprehensive services and built a new type of economic ecosystem. Through the provision of digital services, the construction of online platforms, information aggregation and data sharing, these platforms play an important role in the deployment of resources, the flow of materials and online offices, improving market efficiency and promoting innovation and economic development.

Digital economy platform enterprises form a digital industrial ecosystem through the construction of digitised industrial chains, supply chains and innovation chains, and play an important role in improving the quality of the domestic general circulation and unimpeded domestic and international double circulation. Digital economy platform enterprises are important carriers for building industrial ecosystems, which can effectively integrate discrete factor resources such as manufacturers, suppliers and service providers, and form an industrial division of labour model with data as the core element, network synergy and co-creation and sharing. Platform enterprises are important leaders in building innovation ecosystems, with the ability to breed new universal technologies, and are the core organisations in building industrial innovation chains. At the same time, platform enterprises are an important support for the creation of inclusive trade, for example, the rapid development of cross-border e-commerce platforms has lowered the threshold of international trade and promoted the transformation of international trade from a large enterprise-led, bulk goods trade model to a new model with extensive participation by small and medium-sized enterprises, massive varieties and fragmented transactions.

With the continuous innovation of digital technologies and the rapid development of the digital economy, digital platforms have increasingly become central hubs that bring together interdependent participants in multi-sided markets. These platforms perform key functions such as information dissemination, demand matching, relationship coordination, and resource allocation. In this process, platforms accumulate vast amounts of data and exert control over algorithms, while unilaterally setting and enforcing trading rules. The monopolistic behavior that arises in such settings exhibits characteristics distinct from those found in traditional markets, raising widespread concerns about the adequacy of antitrust regulation in the digital economy. Due to their inherent features—such as economies of scale and network effects—digital platforms are prone to establishing dominant market positions, often reshaping competitive landscapes into oligopolistic structures and triggering "winner-takes-all" dynamics. While platforms can enhance the efficiency of resource allocation by leveraging data, computing power, and algorithms to precisely match supply and demand, their dominance also opens the door to potential abuses. These include the exploitation of market power to analyze and exploit user data, the use of exclusive agreements, and predatory mergers and acquisitions that exclude or restrict competitors. Such practices entrench market dominance, hinder the entry and growth of other players, and ultimately undermine market fairness and consumer welfare.

2.2.2 Data as a Core Element of Market Competition

Data have characteristics such as informatisation, structuring and codification, as well as high initial fixed costs, zero marginal costs and cumulative spillover effects. These characteristics determine that data are significantly different from the factors of production (e.g., land, oil, labour, technology, capital) in the traditional industrial economy. The production and use of data can bring about efficiency gains and cost reductions, thus playing a key role in market competition. The Fourth Plenary Session of the Nineteenth Central Committee formally identified “data” as a new factor of production.

With the advent of the digital economy, data are assuming an increasingly important role in the social production process, which may produce disruptive changes in the existing socio-economic system. The importance of data as a factor of production lies in its ability to penetrate all areas of the economy and society and drive profound changes in production methods, business models and organisational structures. The application of data will improve production efficiency, optimise resource allocation and reduce operating costs, thereby promoting high-quality economic development. With the progress of digital technology, the collection, storage, processing, circulation, analysis and application of data are developing rapidly. Data will become an important bargaining chip for cooperation and competition among enterprises, promoting close cooperation and collaborative innovation among enterprises upstream and downstream of the industrial chain. As the foundation of the digital economy, data elements play an important role in production, distribution, circulation and consumption. Digital economy platforms strengthen their data control through algorithms and other technological forces to raise market entry barriers and exclude market competition. Platforms take advantage of their data aggregator status and their technological advantage in rapidly collecting and processing data, and apply the results of their analyses to their market business strategies in order to gain market influence or the power of a dominant position.

2.2.3 A Set of Unfair Competitive Practices Employed by Digital Economy Platforms

The tactics that online economic platforms may employ in relation to data monopolisation typically involve the use of big data and advanced algorithms to increase market control, crowd out competitors and impose unfair trading conditions on consumers. The following are some typical data monopoly tactics:

- Exclusivity Agreements: The Exclusivity Agreements practice refers to the conduct whereby platform enterprises with a dominant market position explicitly or implicitly compel merchants or users to choose exclusively between their platform and competing platforms for cooperation or transactions, under the threat of punitive measures such as traffic restrictions, search demotion, or withdrawal of benefits. This practice typically produces significant anti-competitive effects. Forced exclusivity coerces merchants or users to abandon other platforms, making it difficult for competitors—particularly small and medium-sized platforms or new entrants—to secure sufficient user or supplier resources, thereby undermining effective competition. Moreover, by locking in merchants and users, dominant platforms reinforce their market dominance, stifling innovation and market dynamism.
- Self-Preferencing: Platforms take advantage of their dominant market position to give priority to recommending their own products or services through algorithmic adjustments or platform rule settings, or to give advantages to their own business in search results, advertisement display, etc., so as to crowd out other competitors.
- Price Discrimination: Digital platforms may implement differentiated pricing strategies based on users' purchase history, browsing behavior, geographic location, and other personal data. Such strategies can result in the same goods or services being offered at different prices to different consumers, potentially undermining consumer welfare and raising concerns about fairness in market transactions.
- Data Blocking: Platforms deny critical data to competitors or third parties, or limit the interoperability of data, preventing other businesses from accessing and using that data to maintain their competitive advantage.
- Algorithmic Collusion (Algorithmic Collusion): platforms coordinate prices or other market behaviours through algorithms, even without an explicit cooperation agreement, and can achieve similar effects to traditional collusion through algorithmic similarity, harming market competition.
- Tying or Bundling: Platforms require users to purchase a product or service along with other specified products or services. This practice limits consumer choice and may force users to accept products they do not need or want to purchase.
- Barring New Entrants: By controlling key platform resources or technical standards, platforms may limit market entry by new competitors, thereby reducing competitive pressures.
- Exploiting Network Effects: Platforms strengthen their market position by increasing their user base to enhance network effects, making it more difficult for users to switch to other platforms.
- Abuse of Intellectual Property Rights (IPR): Platforms may abuse their IPR, such as patents, copyrights or trademark rights, to exclude or restrict competition.
- Unfair Manipulation of Platform Rules: Platforms may establish or modify rules in ways that unfairly restrict the visibility and sales of certain merchants or products, or grant undue advantages to their own offerings.

After examining the potential mechanisms of data-based monopolistic practices employed by online economic platforms, it is important to clarify that our stance toward the use of algorithms in market competition is one of caution rather than outright opposition. We do not object to algorithmic technologies per se or to their legitimate application in commercial activities. Rather, our concern lies in the potential misuse of algorithms to facilitate unfair competitive practices. As a technological tool, algorithms possess a distinctly double-edged nature: while they can enhance market efficiency and drive innovation, they also present significant risks when exploited in ways that undermine fair competition and harm consumer interests.

2.3 Limitations of Traditional Antitrust

Traditional antitrust laws have played an important role in the past decades, however, with the globalisation of the economy and the accelerating digital transformation, traditional antitrust laws are facing new challenges. While traditional antitrust laws usually focus on restricting obvious monopolistic behaviours such as price fixing, market segmentation, and collusive behaviours, some emerging forms of monopoly and market behaviours in the context of digital transformation have challenged the scope of application and the effectiveness of the traditional antitrust laws, which we summarize in the following two points:

2.3.1 Diversity and Hidden Nature of Monopolistic Behaviour in the Platform Economy

In the digital economy era, platform enterprises often operate within bilateral or multilateral market structures. Their reliance on network effects, economies of scale, and lock-in mechanisms complicates and obscures the delineation of relevant markets. Traditional methods for defining relevant markets—such as the cross-elasticity of demand test and the hypothetical monopolist test—focus primarily on price-based substitution analysis. However, these approaches struggle to accommodate the unique features of digital platforms, including free services, data-driven competition, and cross-market interactions. In conventional antitrust law, market share serves as a key indicator of market power. Yet, with the rise of data and algorithms as critical competitive assets, factors such as network effects and user stickiness increasingly challenge the traditional criteria for identifying market dominance.

Meanwhile, monopolistic practices in the digital economy have become increasingly diverse, encompassing emerging forms such as data monopolies, algorithmic collusion, and predatory mergers and acquisitions. These new types of monopolistic conduct are often difficult to detect and identify, posing significant challenges for antitrust enforcement. The covert nature of monopolistic behavior in platform economies is reflected in the following aspects:

Data-driven pricing strategies: Platform enterprises leverage big data analytics and algorithmic technologies to create detailed consumer profiles, enabling the implementation of personalized pricing strategies such as "data-enabled price discrimination" (e.g., charging loyal users higher prices). These practices are often opaque to consumers and difficult to detect, making regulatory intervention challenging.

Cross-market competition and entry barriers: With access to vast data and network effects, platform firms can swiftly expand into adjacent markets, engaging in cross-sector competition. Simultaneously, by controlling data and algorithms, they can erect high entry barriers that hinder the market participation of potential rivals. These structural strategies are difficult for regulatory bodies to identify and address in a timely manner.

Algorithmic collusion: Platforms may tacitly coordinate prices and market behavior through algorithmic pricing and synchronized strategies, effectively achieving collusion without explicit communication. The black-box nature of algorithmic decision-making renders such collusion difficult to detect and prove through traditional enforcement mechanisms.

Killer acquisitions: Large platform companies may acquire emerging competitors or innovative startups with the intent of neutralizing potential threats to their market dominance. These acquisitions often escape scrutiny in their early stages, only revealing their anticompetitive impact after substantial harm to market competition has occurred.

2.3.2 *Broadness and Vagueness of Traditional Antitrust Laws*

The traditional antitrust law covers broad principles, such as the promotion of fair competition and the protection of consumer interests, etc., but lacks clear operational standards and specific legal provisions in concrete implementation, which limits the operability of the law in practical application. Especially in the face of the vaguely defined and complex digital economy platform, the traditional antitrust law is not targeted and too weak in the face of dynamic competition and rapid technological change in the digital market [3]. The problem is that traditional antitrust laws are not targeted or practical in the face of dynamic competition and rapid technological change.

Traditional antitrust law is rooted in classical economic models and typically demands a high evidentiary threshold to prove monopolistic conduct. However, with the rapid advancement of technology, monopolistic behavior in the digital economy has become increasingly covert and complex. Platform enterprises are leveraging ever more sophisticated algorithms and technical tools, while traditional antitrust frameworks have failed to keep pace with these developments. As a result, conventional regulatory instruments and methods often prove inadequate when addressing emerging forms of monopolistic practices such as algorithmic pricing and data monopolization. For instance, platform firms may employ algorithms to implement personalized pricing strategies for consumers, the opacity of which makes it difficult for regulatory authorities to detect and substantiate monopolistic intent or effect. Moreover, the rapid flow and processing of data further obscure the traces of such conduct, posing significant challenges for traditional enforcement mechanisms in adapting to the dynamic nature of digital markets.

In the era of digital economy driven by data elements, large Internet enterprises can use data advantages to easily achieve monopoly in cross-market areas with the help of monopoly leverage, and with the growth of the value of the data volume increasing attributes make enterprises more willing to achieve "data hegemony" through "strangulation" mergers and acquisitions to aggregate data. [4]. The data hegemony is a result of "stranglehold" mergers and acquisitions. It is difficult to adapt to the needs of the digital economy by relying only on the antitrust regulation that focuses on the judgement of specific monopoly behaviours.

In summary, the broadness and vagueness of the traditional antitrust law lies in its overly general provisions in principle, its lack of specificity and clarity with respect to the characteristics of the digital economy, as well as its deficiencies in economic modelling and regulatory tools, which leads to uncertainty and difficulty in enforcing the law in practical application.

2.4 Innovation and Exploration of Antitrust Regulation in the Age of Digital Economy

In the era of digital economy, antitrust laws are facing new challenges and needs, and countries and regions are actively exploring and innovating their antitrust legal regimes to adapt to the characteristics and development trends of the digital economy. The latest developments in antitrust law in various countries and regions are set out below.

2.4.1 EU

In April 2016, the European Union adopted the General Data Protection Regulation GDPR, a statute designed to strengthen personal data protection and privacy rights. The GDPR imposes strict requirements on how businesses process personal data and imposes heavy fines on companies that violate the rules, reflecting a trend towards regulating discriminatory pricing practices with respect to big data.

On 15 December 2020, the Draft Law on Digital Services and the Draft Law on Digital Markets: the European Commission proposed two bills aimed at clarifying the responsibilities of digital service providers and strengthening the regulation of social media, e-commerce platforms and other online platforms. In particular, the Draft Digital Markets Act introduces a "gatekeeper" regime, which sets out a series of obligations and restrictions on large platforms with a dominant market position, in order to promote competition and protect consumer rights. Gatekeepers providing core platform services to merchants or users in the EU are the focus of regulation.

The two Bills were passed and published in full in 2022. The Bills bring a new regulatory "ex ante" regime to the digital market, regulating the digital market and creating a fair and competitive digital environment where companies and consumers can benefit from digital opportunities. From the perspective of fair competition in the market, the Digital Market Act aims to ensure fair and open access to digital services by regulating unfair competitive behaviour of gatekeepers, such as enhancing interoperability between gatekeepers and third-party services, strengthening data sharing with third parties, guaranteeing that pre-installed software can be uninstalled and that default settings can be changed. From the perspectives of user rights protection and platform governance, the Digital Services Act aims to promote the development of digital services towards greater transparency and fairness by regulating the behaviour of online service providers, such as regulating the dissemination of illegal content, strengthening the retrospective inspection of online traders to ensure the safety of products and services, and enhancing the transparency of platforms.

On 27 March 2023, the European Commission revised the 2008 Guidelines on the Priority of Enforcement against Abuse of Crowding Out and initiated the drafting of a Guidance on Abuse of Crowding Out, which is expected to be published for consultation in 2024 and to be implemented in 2025, replacing the current Working Guidance. This is a significant development in the EU's regulatory policy on abuse of dominant position of market power, as the EU's specific regulation on abuse of dominant position of market power (i.e., Article 102 of the Treaty on the Functioning of the European Union) has only one Guidance on exclusionary behaviour, while a large number of regulations, guidelines, circulars, notices, etc. have been issued in relation to horizontal agreements and vertical agreements. As for horizontal and vertical agreements, there is a large body of rules consisting of regulations, guidelines, notices, etc. Therefore, the introduction of the new Guidance will mean that the European Commission will have a clearer regulatory policy and rules on abuse of dominant market position.

The Gatekeeper Regulation: This system is designed to impose special regulatory obligations on platforms with significant market influence, ensuring that they do not abuse their dominant position to restrict competition or limit consumer choice.

2.4.2 Germany

Tenth Amendment to the Anti-Restriction of Competition Act, 19 January 2021: The German Anti-Restriction of Competition Act was amended to adapt to the development of the digital economy. The new act expands the scope of trading objects for abuse of a position of comparative advantage, increases the regulation of abusive market power behaviour by undertakings and updates the merger control rules, with the intention of strengthening the regulation of undertakings with a significant market position in the internet sector. The modifications also include the ability of firms in a competitive relationship to make an assessment decision on their partnership to the Antitrust Authority; the granting of additional investigative powers to the Federal Antitrust Authority, where firms will need to consider whether modifications to their own antitrust compliance standards are necessary, particularly with respect to searches by the antitrust authorities; and the possibility that a firm's appropriate and effective compliance measures will result in a downgraded fine amount when the Federal Antitrust Authority determines the amount of an antitrust fine.

2.4.3 United States

6 October 2020 release of the Report on the Investigation of Competition in Digital Markets: the U.S. House of Representatives Judiciary Committee released this report on its antitrust investigations of the four largest internet companies (Google, Apple, Facebook and Amazon), proposing a series of reforms. The biggest change to the U.S. antitrust laws in 2023 was the issuance of the new Merger Guidelines. On 18 December 2023, the Federal Trade Commission (FTC) and the Department of Justice (DOJ) jointly issued the 2023 Merger Guidelines, replacing the previous Horizontal Merger Guidelines (2010) and Vertical Merger Guidelines (2020).

Antitrust litigation: The US Federal Trade Commission (FTC) filed an antitrust lawsuit against Facebook, alleging that it maintains a monopoly through anti-competitive behaviour.

2.4.4 Japan

Adoption of the Act on Transparency of Transactions on Digital Platforms on 27 May 2020: Japan adopted the Act, which aims to regulate specific digital platforms, increase the disclosure obligations of the platforms, and improve transparency and fairness.2024 Adoption of the Act on Promotion of Competition in Specific Software for Smartphones by the Plenary Session of the Japanese Senate in June 2024, which will restrict giant Internet companies that have a dominant position in the mobile phone software market, by Requires Internet business giants that already have a dominant position to open up the mobile phone software market and payment system operations to relevant competing companies.

Guidelines on the Abuse of a Position of Relative Trading Advantage: The Japan Fair Trade Commission issued this guideline aimed at preventing the abuse of a position of advantage by operators of digital platforms, particularly with regard to the acquisition and use of personal information.

2.4.5 China

In 2019, the Chinese government enacted the E-Commerce Law, which contains provisions related to the prevention and regulation of BDDP behaviour. The introduction of this law demonstrates the Chinese government's concern and willingness to govern online platforms' potential misuse of big data for unfair pricing practices.

On 31 January 2021, the Action Programme for Building a High-standard Market System issued by the General Office of the CPC Central Committee and the General Office of the State Council pointed out that the strengthening and improvement of anti-monopoly and anti-unfair competition law enforcement should "promote the improvement of the determination of monopoly of platform enterprises and the management of data collection and use". At present, the research on data competition in China's academic circles mainly focuses on data ownership and unfair competition, and less on analysing from the perspective of data monopoly. However, as enterprises, especially some large enterprises, are mastering more and more data, it is imminent to analyse the challenge of big data on antitrust.2021 The State Council issued the "Antimonopoly Committee of the State Council's Anti-Monopoly Guidelines on Anti-Monopoly in the Field of the Platform Economy", in which the keyword "data" appeared 18 times, which indicates that data monopoly has become a major concern in China. monopoly has become a core issue of concern in China.

On 7 February of the same year, the Anti-Monopoly Committee of the State Council issued the Anti-Monopoly Guidelines on the Platform Economy, which provide systematic norms for the regulation of anti-monopoly in the platform economy, stressing that anti-monopoly laws and regulations are applicable to all industries, and that all types of market players are to be treated in the same way and in a fair and equitable manner. The guide also clarifies the attitude towards monopolistic behaviours such as "two-for-one" and proposes principles for reviewing the concentration of operators in the platform economy.

On 20 August 2021, China formally adopted the Personal Information Protection Law, which came into force on 1 November of the same year. Although the Law is not a specific anti-monopoly regulation, it imposes strict requirements on the collection, processing and use of data on digital economy platforms, which has a significant impact on the data processing activities of platform enterprises and indirectly involves the enforcement of anti-monopoly regulations.

On 24 June 2022, China made its first amendment to the Anti-Monopoly Law, which responds to new issues in the development of the digital economy, particularly with regard to anti-monopoly in the platform economy. The revised law added provisions that operators shall not use data and algorithms, technology, capital advantages, and platform rules to engage in monopolistic behaviour, strengthened the regulation of abuse of dominant market position by platform enterprises, and optimised the review procedures for concentration of operators.

On 10 January 2023, China began to implement the Administrative Provisions on Depth Synthesis of Internet Information Services, while on 18 February 2024, the State Internet Information Office publicly released the fourth batch of filing information on algorithms for depth synthesis services in the territory in accordance with the provisions. This measure aims to improve the transparency of algorithms, ensure the reasonable use of algorithms, and prevent the abuse of algorithms from causing market distortion or monopoly. Subjects required to file include deep synthesis service providers and technical supporters. This means that not only the direct provider of the service, but also the company providing technical support for it needs to be filed. The algorithms that have passed the filing cover a wide range of fields and applications, such as Scan Almighty, Vivo Blue Heart Big Model Algorithm, TCL Intelligent Q&A Content Generation Algorithm, and so on. These algorithms can operate legally under the regulatory framework after passing the filing. Through the filing of algorithms, regulators can better understand and monitor the application of algorithms in the market, and detect and deal with possible monopolistic behaviour or unfair competition in a timely manner. This also helps protect consumer rights and prevent problems such as algorithmic discrimination and price fixing.

Given the complexity and diversity of the application of algorithms, the history and practice of antitrust law, as an area of law full of uncertainty, suggests that the judgement of whether an algorithm constitutes unfair competition should be based on the principle of the "rule of reason", rather than simply adopting the principle of the "per se violation". In other words, we need to carefully analyse and assess the specific circumstances of the application of algorithms, rather than prohibiting or permitting them in a blanket manner.

Setting a clear and fixed standard of legitimacy for the application of algorithms to market competition by online economic platforms is a challenging task. This is not only because of the rapid changes in algorithmic technology, but also because of the fluidity of the competitive market environment. Therefore, we need a legal process that can accommodate a plurality of viewpoints and allow for full debate to ensure that judgements on these issues are both fair and transparent. Through the defence of both sides, we can reveal the facts, assess the evidence and ultimately form a judgement through procedural law, either in a court of law or in a regulatory body.

In view of this, we expect to be able to explore this area in depth with the power of artificial intelligence technology. By constructing computational models and simulation algorithms, we can attempt to establish more prudent and rational criteria for judging data monopoly behaviour. Such an approach will not only improve our understanding of the impact of algorithmic applications, but also provide a more precise and objective analytical tool for antitrust legal practice. In this way, we can better balance the relationship between innovation and fairness, efficiency and justice, and ensure that data monopoly behaviour is effectively regulated and constrained.

References

1. Xu X-C, Zhang M-H (2020) Research on the scale measurement of china's digital economy--based on the perspective of international comparison. China Ind Econ 5:23–41. https://doi.org/10.19581/j.cnki.ciejournal
2. Zhao C, Ban Y, Li H (2021) The mechanism, path and countermeasure of the new development pattern of dual circulation boosted by digital economy. Int Trade 2:12–18+54. https://doi.org/10.14114/j.cnki.itrade.2021.02.003
3. Zhan F (2020) The antitrust regulation on abuse of dominant market position in the field of big data: from the perspective of methodological improvement. J Shanghai Univ Finance Econ 22(04):138–152. https://doi.org/10.16538/j.cnki.jsufe.2020.04.010
4. Hu J-Y (2021) The anti-monopoly dilemma of data production factors and countermeasures. People's Forum 19:88–91

Chapter 3
Artificial Intelligence and Computational Antitrust

Abstract This chapter provides a comprehensive overview of the integration between Artificial Intelligence (AI) and Computational Antitrust within the broader context of the digital economy. It begins by elucidating the definition, scope, and historical development of AI, emphasizing its interdisciplinary nature and its transformative impact on social and economic systems. As a pivotal enabler of digital transformation, AI enhances automation, decision-making, and efficiency across domains such as healthcare, education, finance, and intelligent manufacturing, while serving as a driving force for high-quality economic growth and governance modernization.

Building upon this foundation, the chapter introduces the economic concept of data elements as a new production factor, examining their role in fostering emerging productivity and reshaping industrial structures. Through the integration of big data technologies, data elements enhance knowledge creation, resource allocation, and innovation across industries, thereby forming the material and theoretical basis for computational governance.

The core of the chapter focuses on Computational Antitrust—a data-driven, technology-enhanced framework for regulating monopolistic behaviors in the digital economy. It defines computational antitrust as the application of AI algorithms, machine learning, and multimodal data analytics to identify and assess monopolistic conduct in real time. The chapter presents a systematic computational antitrust framework featuring human-in-the-loop interactive learning, multimodal feature extraction, and causal relationship modeling. The construction of digital scenarios—exemplified through a detailed analysis of the ride-hailing industry—demonstrates how structured and unstructured data, represented through knowledge and event graphs, can simulate complex business ecosystems and detect anticompetitive risks dynamically.

Finally, the chapter explores the necessity of international cooperation in computational antitrust, highlighting collaborative mechanisms, information sharing, and cross-border enforcement as essential pathways to ensuring fairness and transparency in the global digital marketplace. Collectively, these discussions lay the groundwork for a comprehensive, intelligent, and globally coordinated approach to digital economy governance—one that integrates AI technologies, data-driven insights, and international collaboration to foster a fair, competitive, and sustainable economic environment.

W. Liu, *Computational Antitrust*, Artificial Intelligence and the Rule of Law,
https://doi.org/10.1007/978-981-95-5037-1_3

Keywords Artificial intelligence · Digital economy · Data elements · Big data · Emerging productivity · Computational antitrust · Algorithmic regulation · Digital scenario construction · Knowledge graphs · Event graphs · Human-in-the-loop learning · Platform economy · International cooperation

3.1 Overview of Artificial Intelligence

3.1.1 Definition and Scope of Artificial Intelligence

Artificial Intelligence (AI) is one of the most transformative technologies of the twenty-first century, encompassing a broad range of concepts and technological domains. The term "artificial intelligence" was first introduced by John McCarthy in 1956, with the aim of describing a technology capable of mimicking, extending, and even surpassing human intelligence. Broadly speaking, AI refers to the intelligent behavior exhibited by computer systems that, to some degree, can rival the intellectual behaviors of humans or other organisms. It is not merely confined to executing specific tasks; its true essence lies in the ability to learn, adapt, reason, plan, and solve problems, thereby demonstrating a comprehensive form of intelligence.

At its core, AI is centered around the ability to process and understand complex information, extract useful knowledge from it, and make decisions or take actions based on that knowledge. This process involves multiple stages, including data collection, processing, analysis, and application. Each of these stages requires advanced algorithms and computational techniques to be effectively implemented. Consequently, AI is not merely a technological tool but rather an interdisciplinary field that integrates various techniques and methodologies. The technological scope of AI is vast and intricate, encompassing numerous subfields and research directions.

Our team is currently engaged in in-depth research across several key areas of artificial intelligence, including foundational studies, computer vision, and interdisciplinary applications. Specifically, we have made significant advancements in foundational AI research, such as brain-inspired computing [1] and neural network training optimization [2]. In the field of computer vision, our focus is on core technologies such as object detection [3–5] and tracking [6–8]. Additionally, in interdisciplinary research, we apply AI to areas such as astronomical big data mining [9–11] and intelligent operations and maintenance for rail transit. To better understand and categorize these technologies, we can broadly divide AI research into the following key areas:

3.1.1.1 Machine Learning (ML)

Machine Learning is a foundational branch of AI focusing on enabling computer systems to learn from data and extract useful patterns or knowledge. This learning can be:

- **Supervised Learning:** Systems learn to map inputs to outputs using labeled data [12].
- **Unsupervised Learning:** Systems identify underlying structures or patterns in data without explicit labels [13].
- **Reinforcement Learning:** A specialized form of learning where systems optimize decision-making by interacting with an environment and receiving rewards or penalties [14].

3.1.1.2 Deep Learning (DL)

Deep Learning, a subset of Machine Learning, employs deep neural networks (DNNs) to simulate the connections between neurons in the human brain. DL excels at complex feature extraction and pattern recognition, achieving remarkable success in fields such as image recognition [15], speech recognition [16], and natural language processing [17]. Its ability to learn high-level representations and generalize across tasks has outperformed traditional ML approaches in numerous domains.

3.1.1.3 Natural Language Processing (NLP)

NLP focuses on technologies that enable computers to understand and generate human language. Its applications range from text analysis and semantic understanding to machine translation and conversational systems. The ultimate goal of NLP is to facilitate effective communication between humans and machines.

3.1.1.4 Computer Vision (CV)

Computer Vision explores how computers can extract information from images or videos and understand their content. Tasks include image recognition, object detection, scene understanding, and 3D reconstruction. CV finds extensive applications in autonomous driving, security surveillance, and medical imaging analysis.

3.1.1.5 Robotics

Robotics represents the application of AI in the physical world. It involves designing, manufacturing, controlling, and perceiving robots. Robotics integrates technologies like sensors, actuators, computer vision, and NLP to enable autonomous operations and interactions in complex environments.

3.1.1.6 Expert Systems and Knowledge Representation

Expert systems mimic human expert decision-making processes and typically consist of a knowledge base and an inference engine. Knowledge representation focuses on structuring knowledge in a format that computers can process. These systems have been widely applied in medical diagnosis, financial analysis, and legal consultation.

3.1.1.7 Reinforcement Learning and Decision Making

Reinforcement Learning emphasizes learning optimal strategies through trial and error. In this paradigm, agents interact with their environment to maximize cumulative rewards. Applications include autonomous driving, gaming AI, and resource allocation.

3.1.1.8 Multi-Agent Systems and Distributed AI

Multi-agent systems study how multiple agents cooperate or compete within complex environments to achieve shared objectives. Distributed AI focuses on applying AI techniques to distributed systems for more efficient information processing and resource allocation. The technological landscape of AI ranges from fundamental ML algorithms to sophisticated robotics and multi-agent systems. These technologies interconnect and complement one another, driving continuous advancements in AI. With growing computational power and increasingly abundant data, AI is poised to play a more significant and expansive role in the future.

Additionally, AI intersects with technologies such as robotics, knowledge graphs, augmented reality (AR), virtual reality (VR), and autonomous driving. The ongoing development and integration of these technologies provide robust support for the extensive application of AI.

3.1.2 The Development History of Artificial Intelligence

The origins of artificial intelligence (AI) can be traced back to the mid-twentieth century, as the rapid development of computer science and mathematical theories inspired exploration into machines mimicking human intelligence. While ancient Greek philosopher Aristotle and Chinese philosopher Mozi discussed the concepts of artificial machines and intelligence, modern AI research began in earnest during the twentieth century.

In 1943, Warren McCulloch and Walter Pitts proposed the concept of neural networks, laying the foundation for later advancements in deep learning. However, research during this period primarily remained theoretical. In 1950, British mathematician Alan Turing introduced the famous "Turing Test." According to Turing, if a machine could engage in a text-based conversation indistinguishable from that of a human, it could be deemed intelligent. This test not only provided a benchmark for AI research but also sparked widespread interest in machine intelligence.

In 1956, a summer workshop held at Dartmouth College marked the formal birth of AI as a distinct discipline. At this conference, John McCarthy first coined the term "artificial intelligence," defining it as "the science and engineering of making intelligent machines." Notable attendees included Marvin Minsky and Claude Shannon, who together explored the theoretical foundations and future applications of AI. That same year, McCarthy and Minsky established the world's first AI laboratory, the MIT AI Lab, creating an important platform for AI research.

During this period, AI research primarily focused on symbolic approaches, which used logic and symbolic reasoning to achieve intelligent behavior. For instance, Newell and Simon developed the "Logic Theorist" program, capable of proving mathematical theorems, and the "General Problem Solver" for solving a variety of problems.

3.1.2.1 Growth and Revival in the 1980s

The 1980s witnessed a surge in AI development due to advancements in computing technology and data availability. Expert systems and artificial neural networks emerged as the focal points of this era. Expert systems, which simulate human expert decision-making processes, were widely applied in fields such as medicine, finance, and geological exploration. For example, Carnegie Mellon University developed the XCON expert system for DEC Corporation, saving the company tens of millions of dollars annually.

Simultaneously, neural network research saw a revival. The introduction of the back propagation algorithm in 1986 provided an effective solution for training multi-layer neural networks, fueling the progress of deep learning. Despite challenges such as limited data and computational resources, AI technologies began transitioning from research laboratories to market applications.

3.1.2.2 AI in the Twenty-First Century

The advent of the twenty-first century and the era of big data provided AI with abundant data resources. Significant advancements in computational power and breakthroughs in deep learning algorithms enabled AI to achieve remarkable progress in numerous fields. In 2012, Google's AlexNet won the ImageNet Large Scale Visual Recognition Challenge (ILSVRC) with a substantial margin, marking the rise of deep learning in computer vision. That same year, IBM's Watson defeated human champions on the quiz show *Jeopardy!*, showcasing the powerful capabilities of AI in natural language processing.

In 2016, Google's AlphaGo defeated world champion Lee Sedol in the game of Go, a major milestone in AI history. This event not only demonstrated AI's superiority in complex strategic games but also ignited global interest in AI technologies. Since then, AI applications in autonomous driving, medical imaging analysis, intelligent manufacturing, and other domains have continued to deepen, driving the transformation and upgrading of related industries.

3.1.2.3 AI Development in China

Compared to other countries, China's AI research began later but has advanced rapidly in recent years. With strong government support, China's AI industry has experienced robust growth. In 2017, the State Council released the *New Generation Artificial Intelligence Development Plan*, designating AI as a national strategic priority. Since then, China has made significant achievements in AI research, application, and industry cultivation.

In research and development, Chinese enterprises have achieved notable breakthroughs in areas such as deep learning, natural language processing, and computer vision. Examples include Baidu's Apollo autonomous driving platform, Alibaba's City Brain project, and Tencent's AI solutions for healthcare. Additionally, globally competitive AI companies have emerged in China, such as iFlytek, SenseTime, and CloudWalk.

In application, AI technologies are widely used across various sectors in China, including healthcare, education, finance, and transportation. For instance, AI-assisted diagnostic systems in healthcare improve accuracy and efficiency, personalized learning platforms in education offer tailored resources and schedules, and intelligent risk control systems in finance effectively detect fraud and mitigate credit risks.

3.1.2.4 Applications of AI in Key Fields

Healthcare

AI applications in healthcare include disease prediction, medical imaging analysis, genomics, and medical robotics. By leveraging deep learning and big data analytics, AI assists doctors in making more accurate diagnoses and treatment decisions. Meanwhile, medical robots perform precision surgeries and rehabilitation tasks, alleviating the workload of healthcare professionals and improving treatment outcomes.

Education

AI transforms education through personalized learning plans, online learning platforms, and intelligent teaching systems. By analyzing students' learning data, AI provides customized resources and schedules tailored to individual needs.

Additionally, intelligent teaching systems adapt teaching strategies and content in real-time based on student feedback, enhancing the overall learning experience.

Finance

In finance, AI finds applications in stock trading, risk management, fraud detection, portfolio management, and customer service. AI systems monitor market dynamics in real time, predict trends, and identify fraudulent activities. Furthermore, AI-powered customer service systems offer 24/7 support, enhancing customer satisfaction.

3.1.2.5 Autonomous Driving

Autonomous driving represents a critical branch of AI. By integrating sensor technology, mapping, computer vision, and machine learning algorithms, autonomous vehicles navigate, avoid collisions, and drive independently. This technology improves road safety and efficiency while transforming mobility and urban transportation planning.

3.1.2.6 Intelligent Manufacturing

AI in manufacturing optimizes production processes, ensures quality control, and enhances logistics management. Smart factories automate production using IoT, big data, and machine learning technologies. Real-time quality monitoring and parameter adjustment systems ensure consistent product quality, while intelligent logistics systems optimize routing and inventory management to reduce costs and increase efficiency.

3.1.2.7 Smart Homes

Smart home technologies, an important application of AI in daily life, integrate voice recognition, computer vision, and IoT technologies to enable voice control, scene automation, and remote management. These advancements improve convenience and comfort in daily living while driving the rapid growth and adoption of the smart home industry.

AI is transforming various sectors, including agriculture, energy, environmental protection, and public services. By leveraging AI technologies, these fields can achieve intelligent upgrades, improve efficiency, and enhance service quality, marking a new era of innovation and integration.

3.1.3 *The Impact of Artificial Intelligence on the Economy*

3.1.3.1 Artificial Intelligence as the Core Driver of Digital Transformation

In the construction of digital infrastructure, the role of Artificial Intelligence (AI) is undeniably pivotal. It not only serves as a powerful driver of digital transformation but also provides efficient, precise, and intelligent solutions for building digital infrastructure.

Enhancing Efficiency and Precision in Data Processing

The application of AI in data processing and analysis significantly improves the efficiency and accuracy of digital infrastructure development. Traditional methods often struggle to handle the vast scale of data associated with digital infrastructure, but AI technologies, such as machine learning and deep learning, enable automatic analysis and processing of large datasets, extracting valuable insights and patterns. This automation greatly enhances the efficiency and quality of digital infrastructure projects. For instance, AI can automatically handle data cleaning, integration, and standardization, ensuring data accuracy and reliability. Additionally, by leveraging deep learning, AI identifies patterns and trends in data, offering scientific support for decision-making in infrastructure projects.

Providing Scientific Decision-Making Support

AI's application in intelligent decision-making offers precise and data-driven guidance for digital infrastructure development. Complex data and information often challenge traditional decision-making processes, but AI-based decision models analyze and reason through these complexities to provide sound recommendations. This data-driven approach ensures that infrastructure projects are more scientific, rational, and sustainable. AI models can predict trends and potential risks, offering a comprehensive basis for strategic decisions.

Automation Across All Phases of Development

AI's role in automating processes across various stages—design, construction, operation, and maintenance—provides strong technical support for infrastructure projects. Automation significantly reduces the need for human and material resources while improving efficiency and reliability. For example, AI systems can streamline processes like planning, construction, and quality inspection, ensuring smooth project execution. Furthermore, AI can monitor and maintain equipment automatically, guaranteeing stability and reducing operational costs.

In conclusion, AI is a cornerstone of digital infrastructure development, offering transformative solutions through automation, data analysis, and intelligent decision-making. These advancements not only enhance efficiency and quality but also lower costs, paving the way for more intelligent, efficient, and innovative digital infrastructure.

3.1.3.2 Artificial Intelligence as a Key Technology for Improving Social Governance Efficiency

AI has become a crucial enabler for enhancing efficiency in social governance, providing intelligent, precise, and personalized solutions that revolutionize traditional approaches, significantly improving the scientific and rational nature of governance.

Personalized and Targeted Governance

AI enables tailored governance strategies by analyzing the needs, behaviors, and characteristics of different social groups. Traditional governance often struggles to customize services for diverse populations, but AI's data-driven models ensure more accurate and effective governance measures. For example, AI can mine data to uncover the root causes of social issues and customize solutions for different demographics, enhancing the effectiveness of governance and improving public satisfaction.

Improved Efficiency Through Automation

Traditional governance often relies on extensive human and material resources, resulting in inefficiencies. AI automates processes across all governance stages—from early warning systems and emergency responses to decision-making and performance evaluation—dramatically increasing speed and resource efficiency. For instance, AI systems can monitor societal dynamics in real-time, predict risks, and respond rapidly to crises, minimizing their impact. Intelligent analysis also supports evidence-based decisions, improving the overall effectiveness of governance.

Catalyst for Governance Innovation

The integration of AI in governance fosters innovation and modernization. By synthesizing multidimensional data, AI provides holistic decision-making support, helping policymakers address complex challenges. As AI technology advances, its role in governance will continue to expand, furthering the intelligent and modernized governance framework.

In summary, AI is driving profound changes in social governance, offering intelligent, precise, and personalized solutions that significantly improve efficiency and effectiveness. This transformation not only enhances governance systems but also ensures their sustainability in the face of future challenges.

3.1.3.3 Artificial Intelligence: A New Engine for High-Quality Economic Development

As a core driver of the digital economy, AI's intelligent, efficient, and innovative solutions are reshaping traditional industries and fostering the growth of emerging sectors, accelerating economic optimization and upgrading.

Driving Intelligence and Efficiency in the Economy

AI significantly enhances automation and lean management in traditional industries, such as manufacturing, boosting productivity and ensuring product quality. Additionally, AI enables dynamic adjustments to production plans based on market demands, supporting flexible and customized services. This intelligent approach reduces costs and energy consumption, strengthening market competitiveness and supporting industrial transformation.

Fostering Innovation in the Economy

AI injects powerful momentum into innovation by leveraging advancements in big data and cloud computing. Companies can use AI to analyze market trends and consumer behavior, providing a scientific basis for product development. Moreover, AI accelerates the research and development process, enhancing innovation efficiency and reducing costs. This approach fosters interdisciplinary collaboration and supply chain synergy, creating a robust innovation ecosystem.

Promoting Sustainability and Green Development

AI provides innovative solutions for addressing global challenges such as resource scarcity and environmental pollution. Through intelligent environmental systems, AI supports monitoring, resource management, and emission reduction, strengthening ecological protection. AI also optimizes resource allocation and production processes, supporting green production and advancing sustainable economic development.

Addressing Challenges and Enhancing Capabilities

To maximize AI's potential in driving economic growth, foundational research and talent cultivation must be strengthened. Policies and standards must also be refined to regulate AI applications. Additionally, global cooperation is essential to promote innovation and address emerging challenges such as data security, privacy, and ethical concerns. With the continuous development of digital infrastructure and AI technology, the prospects for high-quality economic development are becoming increasingly promising. AI's deep integration with traditional industries will accelerate transformation, promote emerging sectors, and provide robust technical support for sustainable development. In the future, AI-driven economic growth will reach new heights, achieving comprehensive and long-term progress.

3.2 Data Elements and Emerging Productivity

3.2.1 Economic Perspectives on Data Elements

From an economic perspective, the term "data elements" refers to a specific economic concept: resources in electronic form that participate in production and business activities through computational means, generating substantial value. According to the *White Paper on Data Elements (2022)*, data elements are defined as data resources involved in social production and operations that bring economic benefits to their owners or users. In the context of the digital economy, "data elements" emphasizes the productive value of data in discussions surrounding productivity and production relations.

Simply put, data elements are digital information that can help enhance work processes and create additional value. In the digital economy era, data functions as the new "raw material" that can be leveraged to produce diverse products and services, driving economic growth. For example, a manufacturing enterprise might collect operational data from its machines. By analyzing this data, the company can predict when maintenance is required, reducing downtime and improving production efficiency.

Data elements encompass not only raw datasets but also processed and curated data, such as standardized datasets, data products, and even knowledge or insights derived from data analysis. These elements can be used to design innovative systems, provide valuable information, or develop new solutions. Therefore, from an economic standpoint, discussions on data elements essentially revolve around how data can be utilized to enhance productivity and create greater economic value.

In the digital economy era, data elements have emerged as critical factors driving the development of new forms of productivity. As economic elements, data play a pivotal role in modern economic systems, serving as the foundation for digitalization, networking, and intelligentization. Data have permeated all stages of economic activity—including production, distribution, circulation, consumption, and social service management—profoundly transforming modes of production, lifestyles, and governance.

The value-creation capacity of data elements is evident in their ability to enhance resource allocation efficiency, foster new industries and business models, and amplify economic development. The characteristics of data—its mobility, low-cost replication, and increasing returns—greatly facilitate information exchange, resource sharing, and the efficient operation of economic activities. Moreover, data elements empower other production factors. By integrating with traditional factors like labor, capital, and technology, data can enhance production capacity and drive digital transformation across industries. The scalability, complementarity with other elements, timeliness, and economic externalities of data present new avenues and opportunities for economic growth theories.

3.2.2 Big Data Technologies and Emerging Productivity

Big data technologies, as integral components of emerging productivity, are propelling a qualitative leap in productivity. In the digital economy era, data has evolved from a traditional decision-support tool to a central driver of technological innovation and economic growth. As a novel production factor, data collaborates with traditional elements like labor and capital to lead data flows, optimize the allocation of logistics, talent, technology, and funds, and elevate overall societal productivity.

Within big data, data elements represent the smallest indivisible units—analogous to "atoms." Each data element is defined by specific attributes, formats, and properties. Together, multiple data elements form complete data records. To grasp the concept of data elements thoroughly, it is crucial first to understand the definition of "data." Data refers to the digital representation of facts, events, objects, processes, or ideas and serves as raw, unprocessed material such as numbers, text, images, or sounds. Whether it's personal height and weight, the content of an article or tweet, or a photograph or audio file, all of these qualify as data. However, data alone has no intrinsic meaning. Only through processing, analysis, and interpretation can data transform into useful information. In this process, data elements play a critical role.

Structure and Consistency: Data elements define the structure of data, ensuring the consistency and completeness of data records. During data processing, data elements undergo cleansing to eliminate errors, duplicates, or incomplete information, ensuring accuracy.

Statistical Analysis Foundation: Data elements underpin statistical analysis. By calculating statistical measures (e.g., mean, standard deviation), it is possible to extract summary information, discover patterns, and identify correlations. Techniques such as clustering, classification, or association rule mining rely on in-depth analysis of data elements to provide robust decision-making support.

Predictive Accuracy and Decision Quality: High-quality data elements enhance prediction accuracy and optimize decision-making processes. In machine learning, data elements serve as model inputs. Selecting appropriate data elements and preprocessing them directly impact model performance.

Data elements exhibit diverse types and can be classified according to various criteria. Each type has specific attributes and application scenarios, and the choice of type influences methods and technologies for data storage, processing, and analysis. Table 3.1 presents common types of data elements, highlighting that different types may require tailored approaches for effective handling and analysis.

From the perspective of the platform economy, data elements play a critical role in constructing digital business models. For instance, a ride-hailing platform's user profile comprises multiple data elements:

User ID: U123456
Name: Li Si
Gender: Male
Date of Birth: 1990-05-20
Email: lisi@domain.com
Phone Number: 138xxxxxxx
Registration Time: 2023-08-15 10:30:00
Membership Level: Silver Member
Account Balance: 100 CNY
Frequent Departure Address: XX Road, Chaoyang District, Beijing
Frequent Destination Address: XX Road, Haidian District, Beijing

Each specific piece of information, such as name, gender, or date of birth, represents an independent data element. Together, these elements form a complete user data record, serving as both a digital representation of personal identity and a core resource of the digital economy. Data elements are essentially information generated in everyday life. They can be collected, analyzed, and processed by various entities to produce diverse outcomes in different application scenarios. Consequently, data elements are not merely static pieces of information; through proper processing and analysis, they can play unique roles in various commercial, societal, and even legal contexts.

This study takes a micro-level perspective to explore how data elements can be effectively utilized. It focuses on designing appropriate technologies and mechanisms to transform these foundational data elements into actionable and computable business model scenarios. This transformation enables abstract business scenarios to be presented in a clearer, more structured manner, ultimately forming executable and optimized digital economic models. This process not only facilitates the digital transformation of business models but also provides the technical foundation and theoretical support for addressing issues such as data governance and antitrust in the digital economy.

In summary, data elements are the core resource of the digital economy. Their effective utilization and integration provide a solid foundation for constructing complex digital business models and offer new approaches to addressing governance challenges such as antitrust.

Table 3.1 Types of data elements

Category	Data Element Type	Description
Qualitative data	Categorical data	Data based on categories, such as gender or blood type.
	Ordinal data	Data with order or ranking, such as education levels.
Quantitative data	Discrete data	Countable numeric data, such as the number of vehicles.
	Continuous data	Data that can take any value within a range, such as height, weight, or temperature.
Temporal data	Date and time	Includes dates, specific timestamps, or time intervals, such as birth dates or transaction times.
Textual data	Text	Data composed of characters, such as names, addresses, or product descriptions.
Numerical data	Numbers	Numeric data suitable for mathematical operations, such as price, sales, or age.
Boolean data	Logical values	Data representing logical states, typically true or false.
Hierarchical data	Hierarchical data	Data representing hierarchical or graded relationships, such as organizational charts.
Image data	Image	Data in image form, such as photos or scanned documents.
Audio data	Audio	Data in audio form, such as recordings or music.
Video data	Video	Data in video form, such as surveillance footage or instructional videos.
Binary data	Binary	Data stored in binary form, such as files or programs.
Metadata	Descriptive data	Data describing other data, such as file size, creation date, or author information.
Geospatial data	Geographic data	Data related to geographic locations, such as coordinates or map information.
Network data	Network structure data	Complex data representing network structures or relationships, such as user connections in social networks.
Hybrid data	Mixed data	Combinations of multiple data types, such as user records containing text, numbers, and dates.

3.2.2.1 The Role of Data in Emerging Productive Forces

Data elements play an essential role in the development of emerging productive forces. They drive technological innovation, optimize resource allocation, enable industrial upgrading, promote collaboration along industry chains, and enhance total factor productivity, injecting new vitality into high-quality economic and social development.

Driving Knowledge Production. Data elements accelerate knowledge production and provide continuous innovation momentum for technological breakthroughs. Knowledge production based on machine learning, particularly generative AI applications, can autonomously learn and extract knowledge from massive datasets. This forms a solid foundation for technological innovation, reshaping traditional learning and knowledge acquisition modes. **Transforming Factor Markets.** As a "bridge-type" production factor, data elements integrate other factors of production, driving the transformation and upgrading of factor markets. Digitalization enhances market efficiency, promotes financial development, and improves resource allocation. This helps enterprises optimize resource deployment in an open market environment, reducing mismatches and achieving efficient allocation of production factors. **Accelerating Industrial Upgrading.** The application of data elements accelerates product innovation and technological iteration, driving deep industrial transformation. Data-driven R&D ensures that innovation resources flow to the most needed areas, reducing waste, significantly improving R&D and production efficiency, and enabling enterprises to achieve industrial upgrading. **Enhancing Industry Chain Collaboration.** The circulation of data elements greatly enhances collaboration efficiency within industry chains. By improving information transparency and reducing inefficiencies caused by information asymmetry, data elements facilitate information sharing and collaboration across different industry chain stages. This expands knowledge and information exchange, enhancing overall industry chain cooperation. **Boosting Productivity Through Integration.** The combination of data elements with other production factors generates multiplier effects, significantly enhancing total factor productivity. Deep integration with traditional factors such as technology, talent, and management optimizes business processes, improves service quality, and unlocks the potential of emerging productive forces, injecting new vitality into economic and social development.

3.2.3 The Role and Application of Data Elements in Computational Antitrust

In the realm of digital economy governance, data elements hold significant application value in computational antitrust. First, data elements enable the precise digital modeling of platform enterprises' business models, transforming their operational scenarios into quantifiable digital environments. This process abstracts real-world business activities into computable data forms, providing essential input data for computational antitrust analysis.

Next, the digitized data is fed into computational antitrust models for analysis, leveraging advanced algorithms to deeply examine the data and identify or assess potential monopolistic behaviors. The model outputs must be interpreted by domain experts, who integrate their specialized knowledge and experience to conduct a comprehensive evaluation of the results, ultimately forming a professional judgment on monopolistic practices.

Regarding data types, data elements can be categorized into structured and unstructured data. Structured data typically has a fixed format and predefined structure, making it easily stored, retrieved, and analyzed using relational databases. Such data plays a critical role in detecting discriminatory pricing, often referred to as "price gouging," in big data contexts. For example, platforms can analyze users' historical transaction records and membership statuses to quickly identify potential differentiated pricing behaviors. In computational antitrust, structured data provides robust support for identifying monopolistic practices.

In contrast, unstructured data includes multimedia information such as text, images, audio, and video, which are usually difficult to manage using traditional relational databases. Despite its complexity, unstructured data contains substantial latent value. In detecting discriminatory pricing behaviors, user reviews and complaints—forms of unstructured data—may directly reflect instances of price differentiation. Through techniques such as natural language processing (NLP) and sentiment analysis, valuable insights can be extracted from such data.

In computational antitrust, structured and unstructured data play complementary roles. Structured data often originates from internal enterprise systems such as customer relationship management (CRM), enterprise resource planning (ERP), and user behavior logs. Unstructured data, on the other hand, is abundant across the internet and social media platforms. Although its collection is more complex, it offers richer dimensions for detecting abnormal pricing behaviors. By conducting fine-grained analyses of data elements, regulatory authorities can gain multi-level, multi-perspective insights into market dynamics and identify potential monopolistic practices.

The integrated application of structured and unstructured data supports the construction of more accurate digital market scenarios, aiding in the simulation and prediction of market reactions. This, in turn, provides a solid data foundation for economic decision-making and antitrust regulation. The multidimensional application of data elements not only underpins effective market regulation but also injects new momentum into the healthy development of the digital economy.

3.3 Computational Antitrust

3.3.1 Definition of Computational Antitrust

Computational antitrust refers to a series of technological tools and strategies leveraging digital technologies—especially artificial intelligence algorithms and big data analysis—applied to antitrust governance. Its core objective is to employ automated and precise algorithmic models to monitor and analyze market structures, corporate behavior, and economic effects in real time within the complex digital economy. This enables the identification of potential monopolistic practices, optimization of resource allocation, and promotion of fair competition.

In digital economy governance, as platform enterprises consolidate their market dominance and data control, traditional antitrust regulatory methods face significant challenges. By incorporating machine learning, deep learning, natural language processing, and other AI technologies, computational antitrust can mine behavioral clues from vast amounts of structured and unstructured data. This allows the precise identification of monopolistic practices such as price discrimination, big data exploitation, and exclusive agreements. Moreover, computational antitrust enables real-time algorithmic analysis to predict market trends and corporate competitive behaviors, enhancing regulatory responsiveness and policy-making precision.

Thus, computational antitrust is not merely an innovative approach to antitrust enforcement but also a crucial component of modern digital economy governance. By integrating technology-driven intelligent antitrust measures with traditional legal and policy frameworks, computational antitrust provides a novel technical pathway for establishing a fair and efficient competitive market order through enhanced data processing and algorithmic support.

3.3.2 Data-Driven Antitrust Regulatory Analysis

In the digital economy era, the widespread application of data has transformed market competition dynamics while presenting new opportunities and challenges for antitrust regulation. Data-driven antitrust regulation, which combines big data and AI technologies, has emerged as an effective tool for addressing the complexities of modern market environments. Within this context, computational antitrust plays a pivotal role, enabling the processing and analysis of vast market datasets, including transaction records, pricing strategies, and market shares.

The application of machine learning algorithms within this framework is particularly critical. These algorithms can automatically identify patterns and trends from massive datasets, accurately detecting potential competition issues such as price manipulation, market segmentation, and exclusive agreements. This chapter explores the development of an advanced computational antitrust framework that integrates bottom-up data analysis with top-down economic models and legal mechanisms to create regulatory tools suited to complex market environments.

Specifically, this framework employs machine learning models and AI technologies to extract behavioral clues from massive online economic platform data, focusing on analyzing platforms' pricing strategies and potential monopolistic behaviors. Through techniques such as deep learning, it becomes possible to identify subtle market behaviors that were previously difficult to detect. Coupled with economic models and legal principles, this approach enables detailed categorization of monopolistic behaviors across various scenarios. This provides regulatory agencies with comprehensive and systematic tools, effectively addressing and preventing monopolistic practices in the market.

3.3.2.1 Differences Between Computational and Traditional Antitrust Approaches

Compared to traditional antitrust methods, computational antitrust exhibits significant differences in methodology, technological application, analytical depth, and regulatory adaptability. Traditional antitrust relies primarily on qualitative analyses based on legal, economic theories, and market structures. In contrast, computational antitrust introduces quantitative evaluations through algorithmic models and data analysis techniques. This allows computational antitrust to capture subtle market changes and potential monopolistic behaviors with greater precision and dynamism.

In terms of technology application, traditional antitrust predominantly uses tools from economics and law, whereas computational antitrust integrates computer science, big data analysis, machine learning, and AI technologies. This integration enhances the efficiency and accuracy of antitrust regulation. Computational antitrust, particularly when addressing issues within the complex digital and platform economies, demonstrates superior adaptability and timeliness.

Regarding analytical depth, traditional antitrust often focuses on macro-level market structures, while computational antitrust can delve into the level of individual enterprises or specific transactions. By quantitatively analyzing details such as transaction records and price fluctuations, regulatory agencies can swiftly detect hidden monopolistic behaviors in the market.

3.3.2.2 Comprehensive Data-Driven Regulation

Computational antitrust is advantageous not only for post-incident investigation and penalties but also for achieving comprehensive regulation of market behaviors before, during, and after their occurrence through real-time data analysis and predictive models.

Pre-incident Regulation: Focuses on prevention by employing risk assessment models to predict market trends and potential monopolistic risks. Regulatory agencies can proactively intervene by issuing clear rules and guidelines to ensure compliance and prevent monopolistic behaviors.

Real-Time Regulation: Relies on big data technologies for continuous market behavior monitoring. AI technologies analyze market dynamics and transaction patterns in real time, enabling the rapid identification and mitigation of potential monopolistic practices. Automated monitoring systems allow regulatory agencies to intervene during the occurrence of problematic behaviors, preventing escalation.

Post-Incident Regulation: Targets identified monopolistic behaviors by leveraging big data analysis for detailed investigations. This approach evaluates the impact of such behaviors on market competition and consumer rights, enabling the formulation of legal measures to restore competitive market order. The depth and breadth of data analysis in post-incident regulation ensure accurate identification of monopolistic practices and provide robust support for penalties and remedial actions.

In the face of rapid advancements in information technology and exponential growth in data volume, antitrust regulation encounters unprecedented challenges and opportunities. The limitations of traditional antitrust regulatory methods necessitate the exploration of advanced data-driven approaches to address the complexities of modern markets. Thus, constructing a data-driven antitrust regulatory framework is of paramount importance. The following chapters will provide a detailed discussion on building and implementing the computational antitrust framework.

3.3.3 Computational Antitrust Framework

In this study, we propose a computational antitrust framework grounded in the definition of computational antitrust and aligned with the design process of artificial intelligence algorithms. As illustrated in Fig. 3.1, this framework addresses the complexity and diversity of multimodal data in the digital economy, providing comprehensive technical support for identifying antitrust behaviors through systematic processing and analysis.

The digital economy generates a wide range of data types, including textual data (e.g., orders, user feedback, news articles), image data (e.g., promotional images), and video data (e.g., news reports). To handle these diverse modalities, the framework employs semantic feature extraction algorithms tailored to each data type: textual, image-based, and video-based. By conducting spatiotemporal correlation analysis on the semantic features of multimodal data, the framework constructs a feature map that reveals the relationships among various elements in the digital economy. This map facilitates the transformation of business scenarios into digitized representations.

To meet the demands of practical antitrust scenarios, the framework incorporates a "human-in-the-loop" paradigm of iterative human-machine interactive machine learning. This paradigm integrates domain-specific antitrust knowledge (e.g., classification standards for platform types, definitions of relevant markets, and market dominance) with advanced machine learning algorithms, such as spatiotemporal clue mining and monopoly behavior inference model training. By closely combining antitrust expertise with machine learning model training, the interactive process enables closed-loop validation between expert judgments and machine outputs, enhancing both the reliability of the models and the interpretability of the results.

Additionally, the framework aims to improve the accuracy of monopoly behavior identification and the traceability of clues through its human-machine interactive design. By identifying anticompetitive behavior within extensive digital economy datasets, the framework also supports risk warning and level prediction for potential monopolistic actions. This provides regulators with timely alerts, enabling proactive interventions before high-risk events materialize, thus shifting regulatory efforts upstream.

Computational antitrust serves as a supplement to traditional antitrust regulatory methods, tailored to the digital economy era. It not only integrates computer science and data analysis technologies to digitally define, quantify, and evaluate market monopolistic behavior but also incorporates a human-in-the-loop approach that relies on human expertise for final judgments. The proposed framework addresses novel forms of unfair competition emerging from the use of big data technologies by economic platforms and compensates for gaps in current antitrust laws and

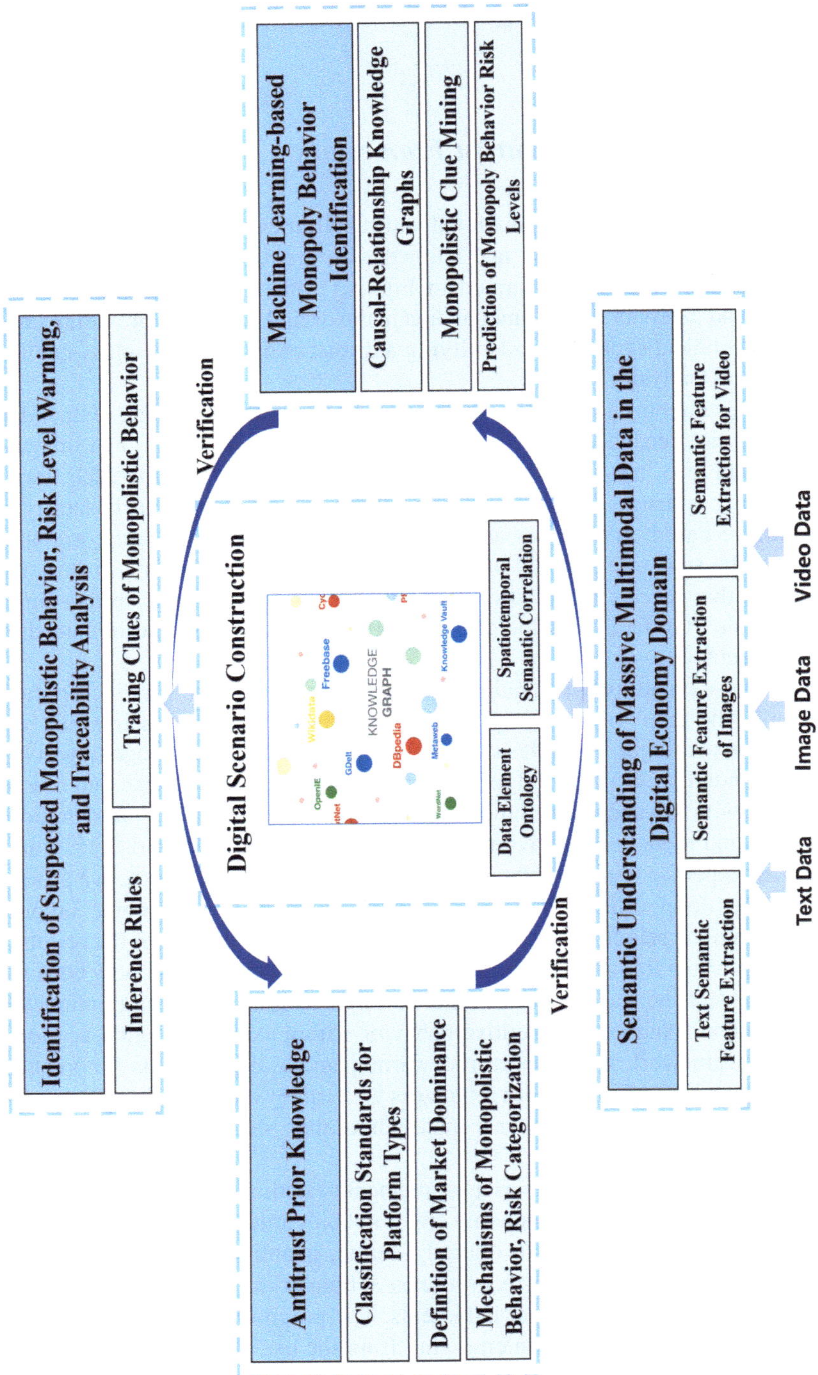

Fig. 3.1 Technical framework of computational antitrust

policies in tackling these new challenges. Through rigorous data analysis and precise algorithmic modeling, computational antitrust offers a more objective and accurate assessment framework for market competition. This approach complements traditional antitrust tools and emphasizes the use of cutting-edge technologies to enhance the evaluation of monopolistic behaviors, adapting effectively to the complexities of the digital and platform economy.

3.3.4 *The Data Foundation of Computing Antitrust Framework: Digital Scenario Construction*

In the study and practice of computational antitrust, data serves as a foundational resource, while the construction of digital scenarios is a key step to ensure the effectiveness of antitrust analysis. By creating detailed digital scenarios, it becomes possible to comprehensively simulate corporate market behavior in the digital economy, capturing complex transactional dynamics and potential monopolistic behavior. This process not only involves the collection and processing of large-scale market data but also requires incorporating industry-specific characteristics to construct digital scenarios aligned with actual business workflows. These scenarios provide more precise support for data-driven antitrust regulation. To further explore this process, the mobility sector is used as a case study to illustrate the specific steps in constructing digital scenarios).

3.3.4.1 Analysis of Business Models in Ride-Hailing

As the platform economy evolves, the mobility market has developed three primary business models: self-operated platforms, aggregators, and carpooling platforms (Table 3.2). These models exhibit distinct characteristics in operation mechanisms, profitability strategies, data collection, and market control, each with unique strengths and challenges.

3.3.4.2 Self-Operated Platforms

Companies such as Didi, CaoCao Mobility, and Shouqi Yueche operate under B2C or S2B2C models, managing their fleets and drivers to ensure service standardization and quality. Their core operations rely on advanced dispatch systems, integrating real-time data, dynamic matching algorithms, and predictive analytics to optimize vehicle allocation and efficiently meet user demand.

Additionally, these platforms embed safety and emergency response mechanisms within their systems, enhancing user trust. Revenue is diversified through intelligent payment systems, dynamic pricing, and collaborations with car

Table 3.2 Comparison of Business Models in the Mobility Sector

Business Model	Carpooling	Ride-Hailing		Aggregator Platform
	C2C	B2C	2B2C	Allocates user traffic to platforms, does not directly provide services
Vehicle Liability	Private car owners	Platform drivers or rental companies	Individual drivers or rental companies	
Pricing	0.3x–0.5x local taxi fares	Economy: 0.8x local taxi fares Premium: 1.8x–2.0x local taxi fares Luxury: 3.6x–4.0x local taxi fares		
Service Providers	Part-time private car owners	Professional drivers (main income source)		
Licensing	None	Vehicle: Online-hailing taxi transport license Driver: Online-hailing taxi driver's license		
Nature of trips	Mutual aid	Commercial		
Representative companies	Dida, Hello	CaoCao Mobility, Shouqi Yueche, T3	Didi, Huaxiaozhu; Aggregators	Gaode, Meituan

manufacturers, such as vehicle sales and leasing, which provide multiple income streams and ensure competitive advantage in the market.

3.3.4.3 Aggregator Platforms

Represented by Gaode and Meituan, aggregators consolidate multiple service providers to deliver one-stop mobility solutions. These platforms excel in technology-driven innovations, particularly in intelligent dispatch systems, dynamic pricing mechanisms, and big data analytics. By analyzing user behavior and forecasting peak demand, they maximize the efficiency of supply-demand matching.

Aggregators primarily generate revenue through service commissions and additional income from advertising and value-added services. Their extensive user data also enables them to offer market insights to third parties, creating further revenue streams while maintaining competitive market positioning through continued technological investments.

3.3.4.4 Carpooling Platforms

Based on C2C models, carpooling platforms such as Dida and Hello leverage the sharing economy to connect private car owners with passengers, providing an economical and environmentally friendly travel option. With a low service fee per transaction (about 5%–10%), these platforms achieve stable revenue due to high transaction frequency. Carpooling platforms enhance user trust through safety measures like trip tracking, emergency assistance, and background checks. By analyzing real-time data, these platforms identify high-demand areas and implement targeted marketing strategies to expand their user base.

3.3.4.5 Digital Scenario Logic Analysis for Ride-Hailing

An in-depth analysis of the ride-hailing business model reveals its role as part of the digital economy embedded within a typical two-sided market, involving three core participants: passengers, platform operators, and drivers. This emerging service scenario demonstrates the complexity of multi-party interactions and the high degree of integration of information flow, cash flow, and service flow in platform economics. This section aims to model the digital ride-hailing scenario and analyze its mechanisms, providing a theoretical basis for constructing analytical frameworks for digital economy governance.

3.3.4.6 Passenger Perspective

Passengers initiate ride requests through mobile applications, select service levels (e.g., standard, premium, or shared), and complete payments electronically. After the trip, they can rate drivers and provide feedback.

3.3.4.7 Platform Perspective

The platform serves as the intermediary, processing trip requests using advanced algorithms to select suitable drivers and notifying passengers of relevant information, including estimated costs. Post-trip, the platform calculates the final fee and deducts a service charge from the driver's earnings.

3.3.4.8 Driver Perspective

Drivers receive trip assignments, follow platform-recommended navigation routes, and ensure safe, punctual passenger transportation. They rely on the platform for navigation and order management, while complying with traffic regulations and service protocols. Earnings are settled through the platform after deducting service fees.

3.3.4.9 Data Elements and Event Relationship Modeling in Scenarios

To analyze the interconnections between elements in ride-hailing business models, knowledge graphs and event graphs are introduced for modeling key data elements and event relationships in the mobility sector. These techniques provide structured representations of complex data, supporting the construction of digital scenarios and unveiling intricate interactions among passengers, platforms, and drivers.

3.3.4.10 Knowledge Graphs

Focus on static relationships between entities, mapping real-world knowledge in a structured way through noun-based entities and their attributes and relationships. These graphs effectively describe fundamental associations but fall short in capturing dynamic and causal features.

3.3.4.11 Event Graphs

Extend knowledge graphs by incorporating events and their relationships, enabling dynamic and causal representation of knowledge. This improves adaptability and expressiveness, especially in capturing temporal relationships and causal chains. Table 3.3 summarizes the main differences between knowledge graphs and event graphs. By combining these methodologies, digital scenarios in the mobility sector can be accurately modeled to support governance in the digital economy.

In the context of constructing digital scenarios for mobility services, knowledge graphs primarily describe the attributes and relationships among passengers, platforms, and drivers, outlining a static relational network. Event graphs, on the other hand, extend this representation to a dynamic dimension by modeling event relationships (e.g., causality, sequence) within business activities, providing a more detailed depiction of the evolution and development of events. Event graphs emphasize temporal order, causal logic, and hierarchical relationships between events, vividly illustrating their trajectories and intrinsic logic. This dynamic nature makes event graphs highly descriptive in complex scenarios, particularly demonstrating innovative potential in identifying risks of monopolistic behavior.

From an application perspective, knowledge graphs excel in representing entity relationships and are widely used in tasks such as intelligent question answering and semantic search. Event graphs, leveraging their unique ability to represent and reason about event relationships, exhibit great potential in analyzing event trajectories, simulating event processes, and predicting future events. For instance, in detecting monopolistic behavior in the mobility service sector, diverse event knowledge can be structured into a continuous event chain based on intrinsic temporal

Table 3.3 Differences between knowledge graphs and event graphs

Feature	Knowledge Graph	Event Graph
Definition	Describes entities and their relationships.	Describes events and their interrelationships.
Representation	Entity-entity relationships.	Event-event relationships.
Types of Relations	Semantic relations, attribute relations, etc.	Causal, sequential, conditional, etc.
Functions & Applications	Search queries, intelligent Q&A, semantic search, etc.	Analyzing event development, inferring event evolution, predicting future events.
Feature	Depicts static, existing knowledge.	Depicts dynamic, evolving events.

logic. When market dynamics change, if a platform's behavior aligns with certain nodes within the monopolistic event chain, this chain can be used to infer the platform's potential future market actions and assess the risk of monopolistic behavior based on its current activities.

In practical modeling, knowledge graphs are first employed to construct data elements with fixed attribute relationships. By extracting the four core entities—users (Table 3.4), vehicles (Table 3.5), drivers (Table 3.6), platforms (Table 3.7)—and their associated relationships, the structured features are analyzed further. In the

Table 3.4 User Data Elements

Element	Example
User ID	Unique identifier for each user in the dataset.
Age	18–50 years
Gender	Male/Female
Registration Time	Year/Month/Day
Occupation	Characteristic variable for user categorization.
Income	Low: ¥2320–4000/month
	Medium: ¥4000–8000/month
	High: ¥8000+/month
Monthly Rides	n rides (specific number)

Table 3.5 Vehicle data elements

Element	Example
Vehicle ID	Unique identifier for each vehicle.
License Plate	City abbreviation + letters + numbers
Seats	4–7
Service Years	1–15 years
Vehicle Price	¥100,000–1,200,000
Vehicle Type	Rideshare, standard, premium, etc.
Availability	Yes/No
Real-Time Location	Latitude and longitude

Table 3.6 Driver Data Elements

Element	Example
Driver ID	Unique identifier for each driver.
Age	18–50 years
Gender	Male/Female
Registration Time	Year/Month/Day
Monthly Trips	30–500 trips/month
Peak Hours Trips	1–31 trips/month
Driving Experience	1–32 years
Driver Rating	0–5 stars
Affiliated Status	Yes/No

Table 3.7 Platform Data Elements

Element	Example
Platform ID	Unique identifier for each platform.
Market Value (Year-End)	¥150 billion
Market Share	30%
Driver Base	19 million active drivers annually
Platform Tier	Small/Medium/Large/Super
Annual Active Users	19 million
Trip Price for Similar Routes	Calculated per kilometer
Financing Cost	WACC formula
Customer Acquisition Cost	Marketing spend per new customer
R&D Cost	R&D spend per team member
Switching Costs	Average cost × number of users switching platforms
Policy Entry Cost	Fixed costs for market entry barriers, regulatory compliance, etc.

mobility service domain, user preferences, platform operating mechanisms, and driver booking habits can all be abstracted into specific attribute structures. This abstraction establishes a foundational data relationship network, laying the groundwork for subsequent dynamic event relationship modeling.

In the context of constructing digital scenarios for mobility services, knowledge graphs primarily describe the attributes and relationships among passengers, platforms, and drivers, outlining a static relational network. Event graphs, on the other hand, extend this representation to a dynamic dimension by modeling event relationships (e.g., causality, sequence) within business activities, providing a more detailed depiction of the evolution and development of events. Event graphs emphasize temporal order, causal logic, and hierarchical relationships between events, vividly illustrating their trajectories and intrinsic logic. This dynamic nature makes event graphs highly descriptive in complex scenarios, particularly demonstrating innovative potential in identifying risks of monopolistic behavior.

From an application perspective, knowledge graphs excel in representing entity relationships and are widely used in tasks such as intelligent question answering and semantic search. Event graphs, leveraging their unique ability to represent and reason about event relationships, exhibit great potential in analyzing event trajectories, simulating event processes, and predicting future events. For instance, in detecting monopolistic behavior in the mobility service sector, diverse event knowledge can be structured into a continuous event chain based on intrinsic temporal logic. When market dynamics change, if a platform's behavior aligns with certain nodes within the monopolistic event chain, this chain can be used to infer the platform's potential future market actions and assess the risk of monopolistic behavior based on its current activities.

In practical modeling, knowledge graphs are first employed to construct data elements with fixed attribute relationships. By extracting the four core entities—users, platforms, drivers, and vehicles—and their associated relationships, the structured features are analyzed further. In the mobility service domain, user preferences, platform operating mechanisms, and driver booking habits can all be abstracted into specific attribute structures. This abstraction establishes a foundational data relationship network, laying the groundwork for subsequent dynamic event relationship modeling.

In the context of vehicle attributes, the number of seats is a key factor directly related to the passenger capacity of a vehicle, particularly significant in scenarios involving family or group travel. The number of seats not only directly influences users' choice of vehicle model but also indirectly affects the overall travel experience. The service life, as an indicator of the vehicle's age and maintenance level, significantly impacts passenger comfort and riding experience. A shorter service life generally implies a newer vehicle, which is more likely to offer a superior travel environment. Vehicle pricing reflects brand value, acquisition costs, or rental expenses and serves as a critical consideration in a platform's pricing strategies and service positioning. Analyzing these vehicle data elements provides essential support for platforms to develop appropriate vehicle service strategies and offers regulatory agencies valuable insights for assessing market competition and service pricing.

In the context of drivers, registration time reflects a driver's experience and loyalty to the platform. Drivers with longer tenures may enjoy certain advantages in dispatch prioritization. Additionally, the number of orders accepted per month serves as a key indicator of a driver's activity level and workload, while the number of trips taken during peak periods highlights their responsiveness to high-demand timeframes. Both metrics are closely tied to the platform's dynamic pricing strategies. Driving experience reflects a driver's expertise and safety on the road, whereas driver ratings, as a direct measure of user feedback, signify the quality of service provided. Finally, the status of being an affiliated driver helps distinguish the nature of the driver-platform relationship, offering a stratified basis for designing dispatch strategies and setting prioritization levels.

In platform enterprises, the market capitalization and market share at the end of the previous year are key indicators for assessing a platform's industry position. These metrics reflect the platform's market influence and competitiveness and serve as critical features for evaluating monopoly risk levels. The number of drivers represents the total volume of service resources that the platform can mobilize, making it a core element of operational efficiency and service coverage. Platform stratification, as an identifier of internal management and operational models, supports differentiated strategies across various business lines. The annual number of active domestic users from the previous year reflects user scale and customer retention, providing a reference for market demand forecasting and resource allocation. Meanwhile, the unit price per trip for the same distance and time reveals the platform's pricing strategy and price competitiveness. Financing costs, customer acquisition costs, and basic R&D costs represent the expenditure structures in capital operations, user acquisition, and technological innovation, respectively, making them critical measures of financial health. Consumer switching costs reflect the potential losses users may incur when transitioning to other platforms, a key factor influencing user loyalty. Lastly, policy-driven entry costs refer to the barriers created by policies and industry regulations for new platforms entering the market, playing a vital role in maintaining fair market competition and regulating industry development.

After using a knowledge graph to depict the characteristics of key participants in the mobility sector, identifying monopoly risks requires addressing the complex and dynamic real-world scenarios. Monopoly behaviors often exhibit significant spatial and temporal dynamics, involving interactions among participants and evolving over time and space. To comprehensively illustrate the occurrence of monopolistic behaviors and deeply understand their underlying complexities and evolution patterns, the application of causal graphs is particularly critical.

3.3.4.12 Methods for Constructing Causal Graphs.

Event Extraction Methods

Event extraction is foundational for constructing causal graphs. This process identifies and extracts critical event elements from large volumes of unstructured data, such as text, images, or multimodal datasets. Event extraction typically involves recognizing event triggers, determining event categories, and analyzing key information such as entities, objects, time, and locations involved in the events. This process relies on deep learning techniques in natural language processing (NLP), including named entity recognition (NER), dependency parsing, and pre-trained language models like BERT, to ensure the accuracy and comprehensiveness of event extraction.

Event Relationship Extraction

After event extraction, event relationship extraction identifies complex relationships between events, such as causality, temporal order, opposition, and co-occurrence. Using deep neural networks and graph neural networks (GNNs), this process maps semantic relationships between events onto graph structures, forming a logically connected event network. For example, consider a platform enterprise that first analyzes user purchasing behaviors using big data, then implements differentiated pricing based on the analysis, ultimately leading to user attrition. These events exhibit sequential relationships: analyzing user behavior precedes differentiated pricing, which in turn precedes user attrition. This approach captures implicit associations and dynamic relationships between events, providing multi-dimensional support for analyzing monopolistic behaviors.

3.3.4.13 Practical Example: Event Extraction and Relationship Modeling

Consider a user complaint about a ride-hailing platform:

> This time using your ride-hailing platform was a terrible experience. As a frequent user of ride-hailing services, I've tried various platforms, but this experience was disappointing. Here's what happened: I worked late and urgently needed to get home, but after waiting for nearly twenty minutes, I noticed the driver was getting farther from my location. I contacted customer service, but their response was slow, merely stating they would 'urge' the driver. The car still didn't arrive. After a long wait, the driver claimed to have misread the address and told me to cancel the order and rebook. I was furious because it was so late, and canceling the order and rebooking wasted my time. Moreover, the car that eventually arrived smelled terrible, and the driver's erratic driving made me dizzy and nauseous. In the summer heat, the driver didn't even turn on the air conditioning. It was a horrible experience.

From this text, the following four key events can be extracted:

Prolonged User Wait

Description: After working late, the user urgently needed to get home but waited approximately 20 min, during which the driver moved farther away.
Emotion: Anxiety, frustration.
Consequence: User contacted the platform's customer service for assistance.

Delayed Customer Service Response

Description: The user contacted customer service, but the response was slow, and the customer service only promised to "urge" the driver without providing a solution.
Emotion: Disappointment.
Consequence: The user continued to wait.

Driver Requested Order Cancellation

Description: The driver claimed to have misread the address and asked the user to cancel the order and rebook.
Emotion: Anger.
Consequence: The user developed strong dissatisfaction with the platform's services.

Low Service Quality After Rebooking

Description: After rebooking, the user encountered issues such as a bad smell in the car, erratic driving, and the driver not turning on the air conditioning.
Emotion: Nausea, fatigue.
Consequence: The user's dissatisfaction with the platform deepened, resulting in a negative experience rating.

Through such examples, the extracted events and modeled relationships can provide actionable insights into platform service issues, supporting more effective analysis of potential monopolistic behaviors (Table 3.8).

The above events, extracted from user review texts, can be further analyzed by constructing knowledge graphs and causal graphs to clarify their interrelations and logical connections. In a knowledge graph, each event is represented as a node, with relationships depicted as edges that form a user experience pathway. For instance,

Table 3.8 Event Extraction

Event ID	Event Description	Associated Emotions	Consequences or Impact
Event 1	User waits for an extended period	Anxiety, Dissatisfaction	User contacts platform customer service
Event 2	Delayed response from customer service	Disappointment	User continues waiting
Event 3	Driver instructs user to cancel the order	Anger	User becomes severely dissatisfied
Event 4	Poor quality of rebooking service	Disgust, fatigue	Extremely poor user experience

the "Extended Waiting" node connects to the "Contact Customer Service" node, which further links to the "Delayed Response" node, illustrating the sequence of interactions reflecting user frustration.

Furthermore, causal graphs reinforce the causal relationships between events. For example, "Delayed Customer Service Response" can lead to prolonged waiting and an escalation in user dissatisfaction. This representation not only highlights the causal dynamics but also provides a structured framework to analyze and improve user experiences.

3.3.5 Computational Antitrust and International Cooperation

With the rapid advancement of globalization and digitalization, the number of multinational corporations and cross-border transactions has significantly increased. While this deep integration of the global economy fosters market vitality, it also introduces new challenges to antitrust regulation. Traditional antitrust frameworks, often confined to analyzing market behaviors within a single country, struggle to address the complexity and opacity of transnational monopolistic practices. In this context, data-driven computational antitrust approaches show immense potential for tackling these challenges, and strengthening international cooperation becomes pivotal to ensuring their efficacy.

In cross-border antitrust regulation, disparities in antitrust laws and policies among countries allow multinational corporations to exploit regulatory arbitrage, evading legal constraints on monopolistic behaviors. To counter this issue, collaboration and coordination among antitrust regulatory authorities worldwide are crucial. Organizations such as the Organisation for Economic Co-operation and Development (OECD) and the World Trade Organization (WTO) have initiated several international cooperation programs to promote consistency and alignment in cross-border antitrust enforcement.

First, establishing mechanisms for international antitrust regulatory cooperation is essential. Regularly convening international antitrust regulatory forums would enable regulators, academics, and industry representatives from different countries to engage in in-depth discussions on cross-border monopolistic issues, share best practices, and present the latest research findings. Additionally, the development of guiding principles for cross-border antitrust regulation would help define the basic positions and objectives of various countries, reducing regulatory conflicts arising from policy discrepancies.

Second, information sharing and joint enforcement actions are critical to enhancing the effectiveness of cross-border antitrust regulation. In the era of globalization, the frequent cross-border flow of corporate data necessitates modern information technology solutions. Establishing an information-sharing platform for cross-border antitrust regulation would enable seamless data connectivity among countries. This approach not only facilitates real-time monitoring of multinational corporations' market behaviors but also provides a robust data foundation for joint investigations and enforcement. Collaborative investigations and enforcement actions, such as those undertaken jointly by the European Commission and the United States Federal Trade Commission (FTC) in cross-border cases, have demonstrated the success of multinational efforts in combating monopolistic practices.

Third, strengthening antitrust compliance oversight for multinational corporations is another vital aspect of global cooperation. Antitrust regulators in various countries need to intensify their scrutiny of cross-border mergers and acquisitions to prevent the formation of monopolistic market positions through consolidation. Moreover, coordinated antitrust investigations and enforcement actions can improve efficiency and deter potential monopolistic behaviors through stringent punitive measures.

Finally, the success of cross-border antitrust regulation relies heavily on professional talent. By enhancing the training and exchange of international antitrust professionals, such as through specialized training programs offered by the WTO and OECD, countries can improve the legal, economic, and data analysis expertise of regulatory personnel, thereby elevating the global standard of antitrust regulation.

In the context of global digital economy governance, the integration of computational antitrust with international cooperation is key to addressing complex monopolistic behaviors. By pooling global resources and leveraging technological tools, transnational collaboration can not only effectively regulate the monopolistic practices of multinational corporations but also promote fair competition and sustainable development in the global economy. The next section will further explore how to construct a data-driven computational antitrust framework to address these global challenges.

3.4 Chapter Summary

This chapter delved into the concept, framework, and applications of computational antitrust in digital economy governance, viewed through the lens of artificial intelligence and data as key elements. Beginning with an analysis of the definition, scope, and development trajectory of artificial intelligence, it examined its profound impact on economic systems, laying a theoretical foundation for the application scenarios of computational antitrust. From the perspectives of economics and technology, the chapter explored the role of data, emphasizing its value in antitrust governance and its importance as a new form of productivity.

By introducing the concept of digital scenario construction, the chapter systematically outlined the framework of computational antitrust, including data-driven antitrust regulatory analysis and the necessity of international cooperation. Ultimately, it proposed a practical computational antitrust framework driven by both data and artificial intelligence, providing robust support for upgrading governance models.

The next chapter will build on this digital scenario framework, integrating specific machine learning algorithms to present detailed technical methods and processes for identifying suspected monopolistic behaviors. By applying these advanced algorithmic techniques, the upcoming chapter will demonstrate how to efficiently mine and identify clues of monopolistic practices within data, achieving more precise monitoring and governance, and providing robust technical support for antitrust regulation.

References

1. Liu W, Yang L, Zhao MX et al. (2025) Towards more discriminative feature learning in SNNs with temporal-self-erasing supervision. Proc AAAI Conf Artif Intell 39(2):1420–1428
2. Liu W, Yang L, Zhao MX, et al. (2025) DeepTAGE:Deep temporal-aligned gradient enhancement for optimizing spiking neural networks. In: Proceedings of the 13th International Conference on Learning Representations. Virtual:ICLR
3. Yang L, Xu Y, Wang S et al. (2022) PDNet:Toward better one-stage object detection with prediction decoupling. IEEE Trans Image Process 31:5121–5133
4. Yang L, Xu Y, Chunfeng Y, et al. (2022) Improving visual grounding with visual-linguistic verification and iterative reasoning. In: Proceedings of the IEEE/CVF conference on computer vision and pattern recognition. IEEE, New Orleans, pp 9499–9508
5. Yang L, Chunfeng Y, Zhongang Q, et al. (2024) Exploiting contextual objects and relations for 3D visual grounding. Adv Neural Inf Proc Syst 36
6. Hu WM, Wang Q, Zhang L et al. (2023) SiamMask: A framework for fast online object tracking and segmentation. IEEE Trans Pattern Anal Mach Intell 45(3):3072–3089
7. Hu WM, Gao J, Xing JL et al. (2017) Semi-supervised tensor-based graph embedding learning and its application to visual discriminant tracking. IEEE Trans Pattern Anal Mach Intell 39(1):172–188
8. Hu WM, Hu M, Zhou X et al. (2006) Principal axis-based correspondence between multiple cameras for people tracking. IEEE Trans Pattern Anal Mach Intell 28(4):663–671
9. Liu W, Cao S, Yu XC et al. (2024) StellarGAN: Classifying stellar spectra with generative adversarial networks in SDSS and APOGEE sky surveys. Astrophys J Suppl Ser 271(2):53
10. Liu W, Zhu M, Dai C et al. (2019) Classification of large-scale stellar spectra based on deep convolutional neural network. Mon Not R Astron Soc 483(4):4774–4783
11. Liu W, Zhu M, Dai C et al. (2019) A deep learning approach for detecting candidates of supernova remnants. Res Astron Astrophys 19(3):42

12. Hastie T, Tibshirani R, Friedman J et al. (2009) Overview of supervised learning. In: The elements of statistical learning:data mining, inference, and prediction, 2nd edn. Springer, New York, pp 9–41
13. Ghahramani Z. (2003) Unsupervised learning. Summer school on machine learning. Springer, Berlin, pp 72–112
14. Kaelbling LP, Littman ML, Moore AW (1996) Reinforcement learning: a survey. J Artif Intell Res 4:237–285
15. Chen C, Li O, Tao D, et al. (2019) This looks like that:deep learning for interpretable image recognition. In: Proceedings of the 33rd Conference on Neural Information Processing Systems. NeurIPS, Vancouver, Canada
16. Al-fraihat D, Sharrab Y, Alzyoud F, et al. (2024) Speech recognition utilizing deep learning: a systematic review. Human-centric Comput Inf Sci 14
17. Luo S, Ivison H, Han SC et al. (2024) Local interpretations for explainable natural language processing: a survey. ACM Comput Surv 56(9):1–36. 2025.8.26

Chapter 4
Discriminatory Pricing Detection Based on the Dual Pricing Model Clustering Framework

Abstract This chapter introduces a novel framework for detecting discriminatory pricing within digital platform economies, particularly in the ride-hailing sector. Building upon the economic foundations of price discrimination, it explores the intersection between differentiated pricing and antitrust regulation, emphasizing the challenges of identifying algorithmically driven discrimination under opaque pricing mechanisms. To address these issues, we propose the Dual Pricing Model Clustering (DPMC) framework, which formulates discriminatory pricing detection as an unsupervised anomaly detection task. DPMC simultaneously learns two pricing models representing discriminatory and non-discriminatory behaviors and employs an iterative "model-learning⋄ data-clustering" process to distinguish between them. The framework further incorporates a pseudo-pricing augmentation strategy to mitigate data imbalance, enhance robustness, and improve detection accuracy across diverse scenarios. Extensive experiments on simulated ride-hailing datasets demonstrate that DPMC significantly outperforms mainstream anomaly detection algorithms and maintains superior stability under varying markup ratios, discriminatory proportions, and data conditions.

Beyond its empirical performance, DPMC exhibits three salient properties essential for large-scale regulatory applications: insensitivity to currency systems, adaptability to evolving platform pricing strategies, and scalability across multiple industries such as e-commerce and food delivery. By providing a generalizable, data-driven approach to detecting algorithmic price discrimination, this framework offers regulators a powerful analytical tool for strengthening antitrust oversight and promoting fairness and transparency in digital marketplaces.

Keywords Discriminatory pricing · Dual pricing model clustering (DPMC) · Platform economy · Antitrust monitoring · Dynamic pricing · Big data algorithms · Anomaly detection · Pseudo pricing augmentation · Ride-hailing platforms · Fair market regulation

W. Liu, *Computational Antitrust*, Artificial Intelligence and the Rule of Law,
https://doi.org/10.1007/978-981-95-5037-1_4

4.1 Introduction to Price Discrimination

4.1.1 Economic Principles of Price Discrimination

The theory of price discrimination originated in the early twentieth century and was first introduced by the Austrian economist Arthur Pigou. Pigou observed that in monopolistic or oligopolistic markets, firms with market power could maximize profits through differentiated pricing strategies. Motivated by this insight, he sought to construct theoretical models to explain firms' pricing behaviors and predict their pricing decisions for different types of consumers. Pigou defined price discrimination as the practice whereby monopolistic firms charge different prices for the same product across different markets or customer categories to achieve higher profits. This theory became the cornerstone of price discrimination research and spurred further exploration of the phenomenon by economists.

Around 1920, Pigou's theory of price discrimination introduced a classification based on pricing methods, dividing price discrimination into three types: first-degree, second-degree, and third-degree price discrimination.

- **First-degree price discrimination** (perfect price discrimination) assumes that firms have precise knowledge of each consumer's willingness to pay and set a unique price for every unit of the product, capturing the entire consumer surplus. However, due to the high costs of gathering such detailed information and the difficulty of fully understanding consumer preferences, first-degree price discrimination is rarely observed in practice.
- **Second-degree price discrimination** (quantity discrimination) involves setting different prices based on the quantity purchased by consumers. This approach is more commonly employed in practice, with examples including bulk discounts and tiered pricing schemes.
- **Third-degree price discrimination** (market segmentation discrimination) occurs when firms segment consumers into distinct groups based on variations in demand elasticity and set differentiated prices for each group to maximize profits. This method is typically implemented through market segmentation strategies.

By the mid-twentieth century, however, Pigou's definition of price discrimination was increasingly viewed as limited, failing to account for the complexity of real-world economic activities influenced by market structures and transportation costs. In 1987, American economist Joseph Stigler offered a new perspective in his book *Theory of Price*. Stigler critiqued the traditional definition and proposed a more precise criterion for identifying price discrimination: it occurs when the ratio of the price of two similar goods to their marginal costs is inconsistent. This refinement allowed analysis to avoid being skewed by external factors such as transportation costs and regional differences, providing the academic community with a more robust analytical framework.

From an economic perspective, price discrimination has become a common pricing strategy in market economies. Fundamentally, it involves providers of goods or services implementing differentiated pricing strategies based on variations among consumer groups. Given that consumers differ in demand elasticity and purchasing power, firms employ price discrimination to further enhance profitability. On one hand, through price discrimination—such as student discounts and senior citizen benefits—businesses can differentiate consumers based on their willingness to pay. This allows companies to more precisely align prices with demand, reducing the inefficiencies caused by uniform pricing, such as surplus for high-willingness-to-pay consumers or the exclusion of low-willingness-to-pay consumers. As a result, resource allocation efficiency improves. Additionally, lower-price strategies enable consumers who otherwise could not afford the product or service to gain access, thereby enhancing overall social welfare. On the other hand the widespread presence of price discrimination has also spurred extensive theoretical discussions, such as those on information asymmetry, the allocation of consumer and producer surplus, and other related topics, thereby enriching the scope of research in this area.

4.1.2 Relationship Between Price Discrimination and Antitrust

In the context of the rapid expansion of the digital economy, the intersection of price discrimination and antitrust issues has grown increasingly complex. Platform operators may engage in price discrimination through personalized pricing algorithms. This practice involves analyzing consumers' behavioral data—such as purchasing habits, digital footprints, and spending capacity—to construct precise individual profiles. Based on these profiles, algorithms predict the maximum price a consumer is likely to tolerate, enabling the platform to set differentiated prices for different users.

When a platform operator with market dominance leverages algorithmic personalized pricing to exclude competitors or exploit consumers—by raising prices above competitive levels or reducing output or quality below competitive standards—such conduct may constitute exclusionary or exploitative abuse of dominance.

From an economic perspective, if a dominant platform enterprise employs differential pricing strategies to restrict or eliminate potential competitors, the behavior may amount to monopolistic conduct. These practices distort market competition, hinder new market entry, and ultimately undermine fairness and healthy development of the market. If the platform's pricing model results in consumers being denied access to the same goods or services under equivalent conditions, or if some consumers are charged prices significantly exceeding reasonable cost without legitimate economic justification, such conduct—often referred to as "algorithmic favoritism" or "price gouging of loyal customers"—may infringe upon consumers' right to fair trade.

Transparency is a critical issue in price discrimination. If a platform fails to disclose the reasons for price differences, leading consumers to make purchasing decisions under asymmetric information, this concealment of pricing mechanisms may constitute unfair competition and violate consumers' rights to information and autonomous choice. Moreover, if a platform uses algorithms or other technical means to restrict consumers' options and conceal more favorable pricing alternatives, such actions could be deemed an infringement on consumers' autonomy, constituting unfair market competition and potentially attracting regulatory scrutiny.

From a legal perspective, the actions of platforms can be assessed against the following criteria:

1. **Abuse of Market Dominance**:
   According to Article 13 of the *Anti-Monopoly Law of the People's Republic of China*, operators with competitive relationships are prohibited from reaching monopolistic agreements that influence market prices or restrict the production or sales of goods. Article 17 further prohibits operators with market dominance from imposing discriminatory treatment without justifiable reasons in terms of transaction prices or conditions on parties under identical transaction circumstances. Additionally, Article 18 stipulates that determining market dominance requires consideration of an operator's market share and the competitive dynamics within the relevant market.
2. **Protection of Consumers' Legal Rights**:
   Under Article 8 of the *Law of the People's Republic of China on the Protection of the Rights and Interests of Consumers*, consumers are entitled to know the true information about the goods or services they purchase or use. Article 10 further specifies that consumers have the right to fair transaction conditions, including quality assurance, reasonable pricing, and accurate measurement. Moreover, Article 18 of the *E-Commerce Law of the People's Republic of China* mandates that e-commerce operators providing search results for goods or services based on consumers' personal characteristics must also offer non-personalized options.
3. **Fairness of Algorithms Applied by Platforms**:
   As per Article 7 of the *Price Law of the People's Republic of China*, pricing by operators must adhere to the principles of fairness, legality, and good faith.
4. **Legal Responsibilities and Accountability Mechanisms**:
   According to Article 46 of the *Anti-Monopoly Law of the People's Republic of China*, operators violating the law by reaching and implementing monopolistic agreements may be ordered by antitrust enforcement agencies to cease illegal activities, forfeit unlawful gains, and face fines ranging from 1% to 10% of their previous year's sales revenue.
5. **International Regulations and Practices**:
   Article 22 of the European Union's *General Data Protection Regulation* (GDPR) grants individuals the right to refuse decisions based solely on automated processing, including profiling, especially when such decisions have legal effects or similarly significant impacts on individuals.

In conclusion, when platform enterprises with market dominance employ differential pricing strategies—particularly through opaque algorithmic methods to manipulate consumer choices—they may engage in monopolistic behavior that infringes upon consumers' legal rights and disrupts market order. Such pricing strategies not only threaten the fair competitive environment of the digital economy but may also jeopardize the sustainable development of platform economies.

4.1.3 Challenges in Regulating Discriminatory Pricing

In recent years, with the rising of the platform economy and the rapid development of techniques for processing big data [1–3], an increasing number of service platforms, such as e-commerce platforms, travel platforms, and ride-sharing platforms, have utilized extensive user data for differentiated pricing strategies. These strategies are tailored according to the varying users' behaviors, preferences, and willingness to pay [4].

In particular, long standing customers who frequently purchase from these service platforms are often subject to higher pricing. This pricing practice is referred to as big data-driven discriminatory pricing (BDDP) [5]. This type of discriminatory pricing, when practiced by enterprises with market dominance, can lead to monopolistic behaviors that infringe upon consumers' legitimate interests and disrupt market order, thereby threatening the long-term sustainable development of the platform economy. Price discrimination in traditional economic systems may achieve Pareto optimality; however, in platform economies, factors such as information asymmetry often lead to inequitable consumer welfare losses. This is particularly detrimental to vulnerable groups whose livelihoods and daily lives heavily rely on specific goods or services. These individuals are more likely to be labeled as having strong purchasing intentions, thereby being subjected to higher prices. The detection of discriminatory pricing largely relies on consumer complaints. For instance, in July 2021, China adjudicated its first BDDP case in which a customer filed a lawsuit against an online hotel booking platform for employing BDDP tactics. The European Customer Center Network reported that 74% of the complaints it received were related to price discrepancies experienced by customers on online platforms. Governments have enacted laws and intensified their scrutiny of data practices to address discriminatory pricing and monopolistic behavior. For instance, the European Union enacted the General Data Protection Regulation in 2016, and China introduced the *E-Commerce Law of the People's Republic of China* in 2019. While these legal frameworks have strengthened oversight of discriminatory pricing, detection remains largely passive, relying predominantly on consumer reports and legal rulings. This underscores the inadequacy of existing mechanisms and highlights the urgent need for more sophisticated tools to proactively detect and address discriminatory pricing.

Current research on discriminatory pricing detection predominantly focuses on understanding the mechanisms and motivations behind price discrimination [6–9]. These mechanisms often exploit consumer data, behavioral patterns, and market segmentation to impose differential pricing, thereby disadvantaging vulnerable groups and perpetuating inequality. Although such practices are frequently justified as market optimization, they can cross the line into discriminatory pricing when the disparity in prices reflects an exploitation of consumer characteristics rather than actual cost differences.

For instance, in the airline industry, ticket prices can vary significantly based on factors such as the customer's browsing history, or willingness to pay. In the consumer goods market, sellers exploit information asymmetry to inflate prices, particularly for minority customers, masking discriminatory practices under the guise of the nature of the goods. These practices not only exacerbate social inequality but also undermine consumer trust and expose companies to legal and ethical risks.

As markets become increasingly digital and data-driven, the harmful effects of discriminatory pricing are likely to intensify and become more widespread. Our research specifically targets the detection of discriminatory pricing in the online ride-hailing industry, with the aim of providing insights that can be applied to other sectors where such practices are prevalent.

4.2 Identifying Discriminatory Pricing Behavior through Price Pattern Clustering Learning

4.2.1 Problem Definition

In this section, we formally define the problem we aim to solve by providing the concept of discriminatory pricing and formulating the identification process of it under the background of ride-hailing.

Definition 1 (Discriminatory Pricing)
Let $D = \{(x_i, p_i)\}_{i=1}^{N}$ denote a batch of N ride-hailing orders, where x_i represents the detailed information of the i-th order (including trip distance, weather, etc.), and p_i is the actual price paid by the customer. We use $\mathrm{F}(x_i)$ to represent the honest price calculated by the standard pricing algorithm $\mathrm{F}(\cdot)$. If the actual price p_i exceeds the honest price by a significant percentage w, i.e.,

$$p_i \geq \mathcal{F}(x_i) \cdot (1 + w),$$

this is defined as a case of discriminatory pricing.

Definition 2 (Discriminatory Pricing Detection)
We aim to develop a classification algorithm to detect the case when discriminatory pricing happens. We call this problem discriminatory pricing detection. Specifically, given a set of ride-hailing orders $D = \{(x_i, p_i)\}_{i=1}^{N}$ defined above, the developed algorithm categorizes the order data into two groups: $D_d = \{(x_i, p_i) | r_i = 1\}$ for orders with discriminatory pricing, and $D_{nd} = \{(x_i, p_i) | r_i = 0\}$ for those without discriminatory pricing (r_i denotes the classification result for the i-th order (x_i, p_i). Although we discuss this problem in the scenario of ride-hailing, the developed system is agnostic to the platforms' pricing algorithm $\mathrm{F}(\cdot)$, the markup percentage w, and the actual number of orders with discriminatory pricing.

4.2.2 Dataset Construction for Digital Scenarios

A direct approach to identifying discriminatory pricing behavior involves comparing a platform's operational data, such as order data, with its pricing strategy. However, ride-hailing companies often withhold such data on the grounds of protecting user privacy and trade secrets, substantially hindering efforts to detect discriminatory pricing. Moreover, the opacity and variability of pricing strategies across different ride-hailing platforms, coupled with the widespread adoption of dynamic pricing, pose significant challenges to monitoring discriminatory pricing practices in real time.

To overcome these hurdles, we initiate our study by developing a comprehensive ride-hailing order dataset that mimics the pricing strategies of major online ride-hailing platforms, incorporating various factors such as vehicle type, peak hours, weather conditions, etc. This dataset encompasses a wide range of pricing scenarios and discriminatory settings. Table 4.1 outlines the key informational factors that make up this dataset. Developed in accordance with the dynamic pricing algorithms detailed in the following part, this dataset includes a variety of markup percentages (w) and proportions of discriminatory pricing (m). Specifically, it consists of four markup percentages: 5%, 10%, 15%, and 20%, each with discriminatory pricing

Table 4.1 Key information influencing pricing strategy in online ride-hailing

Information	Value type	Description
Vehicle type	String	The type of vehicle used for the trip.
Carpooling	Boolean	Whether the trip is a carpool.
Peak hours	Boolean	Whether the trip occurs during peak traffic hours.
Weather	Boolean	Whether the trip occurs during rainy or snowy conditions.
Nighttime	Boolean	Whether the trip occurs during nighttime hours, specifically from 11:00 PM to 5:00 AM the next morning.
Distance to passenger	Float	The distance between the driver and the passenger after the order is accepted.
Trip distance	Float	The unit in km of the trip.
Driver wait time	Integer	The waiting time (in seconds) the driver waits at the pickup location.
Price	Float	The total cost of the trip, charged in RMB.
User order time	DateTime	The time when the user place the order.
Driver arrival time	DateTime	The time the driver arrives at the pickup location.
Number of passengers	Integer	The total number of passengers present in a vehicle during the carpooling.
Order duration	Integer	The duration of the order, measured in seconds (s).
Wait time for order	Integer	The wait time in seconds (s) from order placement to driver acceptance.

proportions ranging from 1% to 30%. Each configuration of w and m encompasses 100,000 orders, allowing for comprehensive analyses under diverse scenarios.

The detailed strategy is depicted in Fig. 4.1. Concretely, a different pricing strategy is generally adopted for different scenarios to reflect the corresponding practical operational cost. Concretely, a different pricing strategy is generally adopted for different scenarios to reflect the corresponding practical operational cost. The standard daytime pricing strategy denoted as $F^{(1)}$, establishes the base fare structure for trips. It specifies one-off fees b for distances up to $k = 3$ kilometers and price per kilometer (λ) for distances beyond this initial threshold. For trips exceeding 15 kilometers, the fare for the additional distance is adjusted by a distance coefficient (ρ), effectively increasing the per-kilometer charge for longer trips. If a driver's order acceptance time t_{ord} falls between 11 PM and 5 AM, we define this as the nighttime period. For rides during these hours, the pricing strategy ($F^{(2)}$) includes a nighttime pricing factor (β), which is applicable to trips of 20 kilometers or less.

For distances exceeding 20 kilometers, a night service fee is added to the standard nighttime fare for each kilometer beyond this limit, to account for the reduced availability and higher operational costs during these hours. Additionally, during peak traffic hours (from 7 AM to 9 AM and from 5 PM to 7 PM), a peak pricing factor (α) is applied to the base fare ($F^{(1)}$) to accommodate increased demand and congestion. In response to extreme weather conditions, the pricing strategy ($F^{(3)}$) builds upon ($F^{(2)}$) by incorporating a weather pricing factor (γ). This factor increases the fares to offset the additional operational costs incurred during adverse weather conditions.

The long-distance pickup pricing strategy ($F^{(4)}$) is implemented when the initial distance between the driver and the customer $d > 3$ kilometers. This strategy

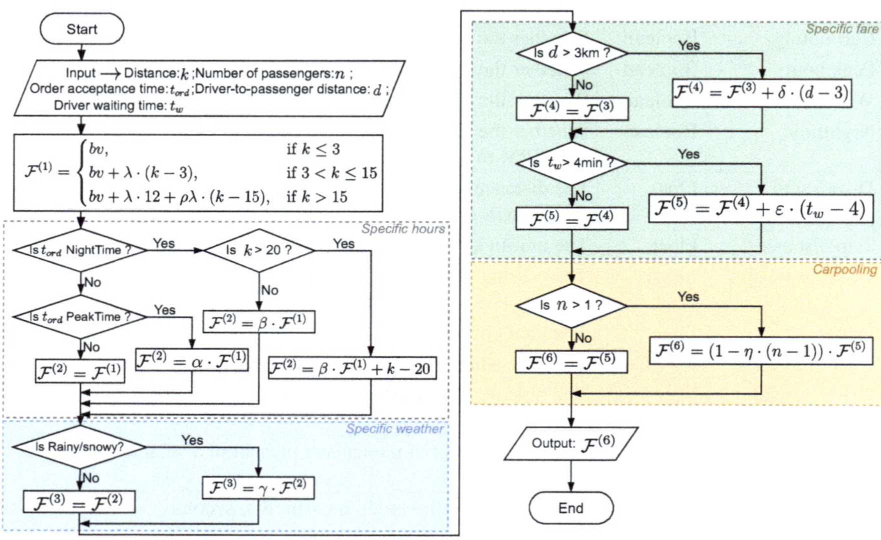

Fig. 4.1 Flowchart of dynamic pricing strategy

introduces a dispatch pricing factor (δ) to encourage drivers to accept these longer pickup assignments and compensate for the extra travel required. If a driver arrives at the designated pickup location and has to wait $t_w > 4$ minutes for the customer to arrive, a waiting fee is charged according to ($F^{(5)}$), with (ϵ) representing the waiting pricing factor. This fee compensates the driver for the additional waiting time. For carpool services ($F^{(6)}$), the fare per passenger is adjusted based on the number of occupants (n) and a carpool pricing factor (η). This pricing strategy ensures that the total cost reflects the cost-sharing benefits of carpooling, making it an economical option for passengers while maintaining profitability for drivers. Finally, based on Definition 1, by setting various markup percentages (w) and discriminatory pricing proportions (m), we have constructed various discriminatory pricing scenarios using the output from the standard pricing algorithm. This method not only effectively simulates real-world ride-hailing pricing algorithms but also provides an essential experimental database for research on discriminatory pricing detection.

We conducted a multifaceted visualization analysis of the data to thoroughly explore its features and underlying patterns. Figure 4.2a illustrates the workflow for identifying discriminatory pricing behavior in the context of ride-hailing business scenarios. This figure demonstrates how real-world business scenarios are translated into digital contexts, enabling the construction of corresponding ride-hailing order datasets. These datasets are then fed into our proposed Dual Pricing Model Clustering (DPMC) learning model (discussed in detail in Sect. 4.2.3 section) to detect discriminatory pricing practices. Figure 4.2b exhibits the histogram distribution of order prices for a specific scenario with $w = 10\%$ and $m = 10\%$. The substantial overlap between discriminatory and non-discriminatory pricing orders suggests that price alone does not suffice to distinguish between them. In Fig. 4.2c, a two-dimensional scatter plot illustrates the relationship between trip distance and price for a random sample of 400 orders. The discriminatory and non-discriminatory pricing orders show considerable overlap on the two-dimensional plane of trip distance

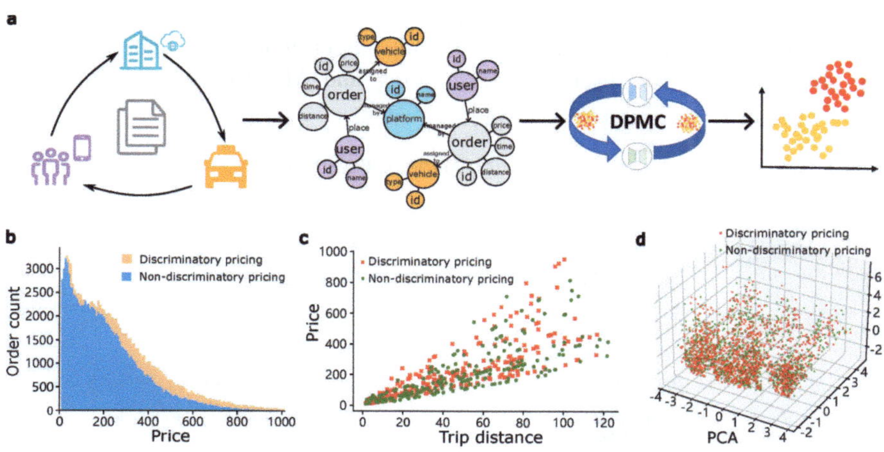

Fig. 4.2 Flowchart of dynamic pricing strategy

and price, remaining difficult to separate. Further, we encode the entire order information into high-dimensional features and apply Principal Component Analysis (PCA) to reduce the features to three dimensions for visualization. As shown in Fig. 4.2d, the order data continues to show substantial overlap in the three-dimensional space, indicating persistent challenges in segregating discriminatory from non-discriminatory pricing orders solely based on observable data. These findings underscore the complexity of directly utilizing order data for discriminatory pricing detection and highlight the necessity to delve deeper into the underlying pricing strategies to effectively identify discriminatory practices. Based on this dataset, discriminatory pricing detection can be conceptualized as an anomaly detection task, aiming to identify data that deviate significantly from standard pricing norms. However, traditional anomaly detection algorithms typically assume a known proportion of anomalies, a requirement that is problematic in the ride-hailing context, where the exact proportion of discriminatory pricing orders within large datasets is often unknown. The opaque nature of pricing strategies further complicates the challenges in discriminatory pricing detection.

4.2.3 Dual Pricing Model Clustering Framework

Based on the above analysis, discriminatory pricing detection can be conceptualized as an anomaly detection task in our research. Compared with common anomaly detection tasks, discriminatory pricing detection is more challenging considering (1) the opaque nature of the pricing strategies used by ride-hailing platforms and (2) the difficulty in quantifying their discriminatory pricing overcharges. To solve discriminatory pricing detection under these challenges, we propose a novel framework named Dual Pricing Model Clustering (DPMC), as illustrated in Fig. 4.3.

The framework effectively segments order data into discriminatory and non-discriminatory pricing groups by leveraging pricing models learned online from order data. Specifically, we develop two pricing models to learn the underlying pricing strategies: M_d for discriminatory pricing and M_{nd} for non-discriminatory

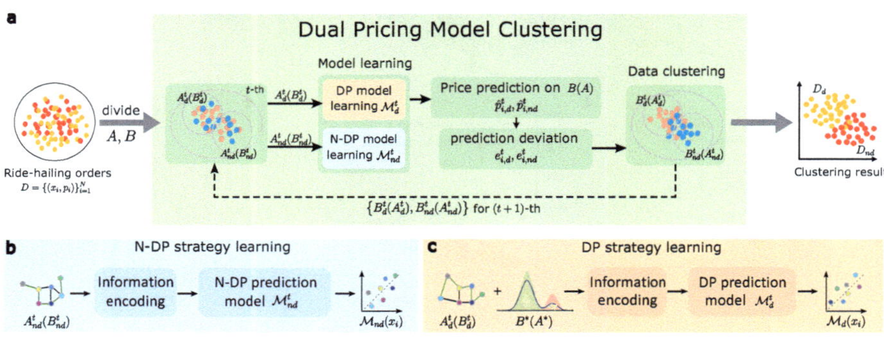

Fig. 4.3 The overall framework for discriminatory pricing detection

pricing. These models take order information as input to estimate order prices under their respective pricing strategies. Since there are no order data directly labeled with pricing strategies, our DPMC method employs a cyclical process of **"model learning→data clustering"** to effectively learn the pricing models.

The DPMC method initially divides the order dataset into two equal-sized subsets, which alternate roles between model learning and data clustering over multiple rounds.

Each round involves training the pricing models using the subset that has been grouped into discriminatory and non-discriminatory clusters from the previous round, and then applying these models to the clustering of the other subset. The absolute differences between the actual and predicted prices are calculated to categorize orders as discriminatory or non-discriminatory pricing. This iterative "model learning→data clustering" process is repeated for a predefined number of rounds on the two subsets, progressively refining the pricing models to better align with the actual pricing strategies, thereby enhancing the accuracy of detecting discriminatory pricing. Finally, the learned pricing models are applied to the entire dataset to classify all orders.

To enhance detection capabilities, especially in scenarios where discriminatory pricing is rare, we further introduce a pseudo-pricing augmentation strategy, which augments the order data by statistically estimating the markup percentage of discriminatory pricing. This strategy mitigates data imbalance and improves model learning efficiency, thus strengthening DPMC's ability to detect discriminatory pricing across various data distributions.

Our experimental results demonstrate that the DPMC framework excels in detecting discriminatory pricing with high accuracy and robustness across diverse scenarios, significantly outperforming existing mainstream anomaly detection algorithms. Although initially developed for ride-hailing contexts, the DPMC framework can also be applied to other service domains like e-commerce and travel services, where it can help enforce fair pricing regulations and mitigate discriminatory practices. This adaptability underscores its potential to influence a wide range of platform economies, promoting equitable pricing practices and enhancing antitrust monitoring.

4.2.3.1 Dual Pricing Model Clustering Learning

Given a dataset of \$N\$ orders, denoted as $D = \{(x_i, p_i)\}_{i=1}^{N}$, our approach is designed to produce binary classification results $\{r_i \mid r_i \in \{0,1\}\}_{i=1}^{N}$, categorizing each order into discriminatory pricing ($r_i = 1$) or non-discriminatory pricing ($r_i = 0$) (in the problem definition section). To accomplish this, we develop two pricing models for learning different pricing strategies: M_d for discriminatory pricing and M_{nd} for non-discriminatory pricing. The pricing models take the order information x_i as input and estimate the order price under their respective pricing strategies, i.e., $M_d(x_i)$ and $M_{nd}(x_i)$. Since direct data corresponding to these pricing strategies is unavailable, our DPMC method introduces an iterative process of "modeling learning → data clustering" to facilitate the effective learning of pricing models.

In our methodology, the dataset D is initially split randomly into two equal-sized subsets, A and B, alternately used for model learning and data clustering across multiple learning rounds. For example, in the t-th learning round, subset A—previously grouped into discriminatory (A_d^{t-1}) and non-discriminatory (A_{nd}^{t-1}) pricing clusters—is used to train the two pricing models $\mathcal{M}_d^t$ and $\mathcal{M}_{nd}^t$.

These models are then applied to subset B to predict the price per order under different pricing strategies:

$$\hat{p}_{i,d}^t = \mathcal{M}_d^t\left(x_i\right), \quad \hat{p}_{i,nd}^t = \mathcal{M}_{nd}^t\left(x_i\right).$$

We calculate the absolute differences between the actual order price p_i and the above model-predicted prices:

$$e_{i,d}^t = \left|p_i - \hat{p}_{i,d}^t\right|, \quad e_{i,nd}^t = \left|p_i - \hat{p}_{i,nd}^t\right|.$$

These differences essentially measure how closely each order aligns with different pricing strategies. Let B_d^t and B_{nd}^t denote the discriminatory and non-discriminatory pricing clusters for subset B at the current t-th round, respectively. By comparing the above differences, we determine each order (x_i, p_i) in subset B as discriminatory or non-discriminatory pricing and assign it to the corresponding pricing cluster:

$$\left(x_i, p_i\right) \in \begin{cases} B_d^t, & \text{if} e_{i,d}^t < e_{i,nd}^t \\ B_{nd}^t, & \text{otherwise.} \end{cases}$$

In the following (i + 1)-th round, the roles of subsets A and B are reversed: subset B (with clustering results B_d^t and B_{nd}^t) is used for retraining the pricing models, and the updated models are then applied to subset A for data clustering.

Algorithm 1 Dual Pricing Model Clustering

Input: Dataset $D = \{(x_i, p_i)\}_{i=1}^{N}$ (where x_i represents order information and p_i denotes the order price)
Output: $D_d = \{(x_i, p_i) \mid r_i = 1\}$ and $D_{nd} = \{(x_i, p_i) \mid r_i = 0\}$, representing discriminatory and non-discriminatory pricing orders, respectively.

Divide dataset D into two subsets with equal number of orders: A and B.
for $t = 1$ to T **do**
  Model Learning:
  The subsets A and B are alternately used for model learning and data clustering over T rounds. For simplicity, here we describe using A for model learning and B for data clustering.
  if t=1 **then**
    Randomly split A into A_{nd}^0 for non-discriminatory pricing and A_d^0 for discriminatory pricing.
    Train pricing models $\mathcal{M}_{nd}^1$ and $\mathcal{M}_d^1$ on A_{nd}^0 and A_d^0, respectively.
  else
    A has been grouped into A_{nd}^{t-1} and A_d^{t-1} based on Equation (4) in the previous $t-1$ round.
    Train pricing models $\mathcal{M}_{nd}^t$ and $\mathcal{M}_d^t$ on A_{nd}^{t-1} and A_d^{t-1}, respectively.
  end if
  Data clustering:
  for each order $(x_i, p_i) \in B$ **do**
    Compute predicted prices: $\hat{p}_{i,d}^t = \mathcal{M}_d^t(x_i)$ and $\hat{p}_{i,nd}^t = \mathcal{M}_{nd}^t(x_i)$.
    Compute absolute differences: $e_{i,d}^t = |p_i - \hat{p}_{i,d}^t|$ and $e_{i,nd}^t = |p_i - \hat{p}_{i,nd}^t|$.
    Compute relative deviation: $R_i = \frac{|p_i - \hat{p}_{i,nd}^t|}{\hat{p}_{i,nd}^t}$.
    if $e_{i,d}^t < e_{i,nd}^t$ **then**
      Assign (x_i, p_i) to B_d^t.
    else
      Assign (x_i, p_i) to B_{nd}^t.
    end if
  end for
  Pseudo-pricing augmentation:
  Estimate the distribution of R_i using a kernel density estimator $\hat{f}(x) = \frac{1}{n_B \cdot h} \sum_{i=1}^{n_B} K\left(\frac{x - R_i}{h}\right)$.
  Estimate the w^* based on $\hat{f}(x)$.
  Construct a set of pseudo-pricing orders B^* based on the estimated w^* (see Equation (8)) for the next round of model training.
  Swap the roles of A and B in the next round.
end for
Classify the entire order dataset D**:**
for each $(x_i, p_i) \in D$ **do**
  Apply pricing models $\mathcal{M}_d^T$ and $\mathcal{M}_{nd}^T$ to compute price predictions and differences (see Equations (2) and (3)).
  if $e_{i,d}^T < e_{i,nd}^T$ **then**
    $r_i = 1$ (discriminatory pricing).
  else
    $r_i = 0$ (non-discriminatory pricing).
  end if
end for
return $D_d = \{(x_i, p_i) \mid r_i = 1\}$ and $D_{nd} = \{(x_i, p_i) \mid r_i = 0\}$.

The details of this learning and clustering process are illustrated in Algorithm1. For the first learning round, we randomly split subset A to form two pricing clusters A_d^1 and A_{nd}^1 for pricing model training.

This iterative procedure is repeated for a predefined number T of learning rounds, with model training and data clustering mutually reinforcing each other, thereby improving the accuracy in identifying orders with discriminatory pricing. The final pricing models are applied to the whole order data D to predict prices $\hat{p}_{i,d}^T$ and $\hat{p}_{i,nd}^T$, calculate price differences $e_{i,d}^T$ and $e_{i,nd}^T$, and classify orders as:

$$r_i = \begin{cases} 1, & \text{if} e_{i,d}^T < e_{i,nd}^T \\ 0, & \text{otherwise.} \end{cases}$$

Thus, the order dataset is categorized into two groups: $D_d = \{(x_i, p_i) | r_i = 1\}$ indicating discriminatory pricing and $D_{nd} = \{(x_i, p_i) | r_i = 0\}$ indicating non-discriminatory pricing.

4.2.4 Data Preprocessing and Evaluation Metrics

To transform the order information of the constructed ride-hailing dataset into a form that can be efficiently processed by algorithms, we undertake extensive data preprocessing efforts focused on price-related features. This step is crucial to ensure the model's high accuracy and reliability, fulfilling the specific data format requirements of the algorithms. For categorical data, such as vehicle types (including "multi-purpose vehicle", "tailored taxi", etc.), we applied the one-hot encoding method. This approach transforms categorical features into a numerical format, facilitating their processing by algorithms. For example, with four types of vehicles, a "multi-purpose vehicle" would be encoded as [1, 0, 0, 0], and a "tailored taxi" as [0, 1, 0, 0]. Such transformation allows the model to distinctly differentiate between the categories.

Regarding time features that exhibit periodicity (such as the passenger boarding time), which have cyclic behavior throughout a day or a specific day of the week, we employed a specialized encoding technique to address this characteristic. To effectively capture the continuity and periodicity of time, sine and cosine encoding methods were used. This method projects time points onto a unit circle, not only preserving the unique attributes of time data but also assisting the model in leveraging this information for more accurate predictive analysis. The mathematical expression for this method is as follows:

$$x_{\sin} = \sin\left(\frac{2\pi x}{T}\right), \quad x_{\cos} = \cos\left(\frac{2\pi x}{T}\right),$$

where x denotes a specific time value, and T represents the time period (e.g., 24 hours for a day, 7 days for a week). This approach accurately represents time features and captures their inherent periodicity. The preprocessing of numerical data was performed using the Z-score normalization, which adjusts the feature distribution to have a mean of 0 and a standard deviation of 1, aligning it with the standard normal distribution. Normalizing numerical data is vital for model training, as it facilitates faster model convergence. The formula for Z-score normalization is as follows:

$$z = \frac{x - \mu}{\sigma},$$

where x is the original data point, μ is the mean of the dataset, and σ is the standard deviation.

The F1-score is a statistical metric used to measure the harmonic mean of the accuracy of a binary classification model, taking into account both the precision and recall of the model. The formula for calculating the F1-score is:

$$F1 = 2 \times \frac{\text{Precision} \times \text{Recall}}{\text{Precision} + \text{Recall}},$$

where precision is the proportion of orders correctly predicted as the positive class (discriminatory pricing orders) out of the total number of orders predicted as the positive class, calculated as:

$$\text{Precision} = \frac{TP}{TP + FP}.$$

Recall is the proportion of orders correctly predicted as the positive class out of all actual positive class orders, calculated as:

$$\text{Recall} = \frac{TP}{TP + FN}.$$

Here, TP (True Positives) represents the number of orders correctly predicted as discriminatory pricing, FP (False Positives) represents the number of non-discriminatory pricing orders incorrectly predicted as discriminatory pricing, and FN (False Negatives) represents the number of discriminatory pricing orders not predicted. The F1-score ranges from 0 to 1, with higher scores indicating better model performance, particularly useful when dealing with imbalanced datasets as it provides a more robust performance metric than precision or recall alone.

4.2.5 *Analysis of Experimental Results*

4.2.5.1 Discriminatory Pricing Detection Performance

Discriminatory pricing detection can be conceptualized as an anomaly detection task in our research. We evaluate prominent anomaly detection algorithms in comparison with our Dual Pricing Model Clustering (DPMC) framework, which includes a default version with the pseudo-pricing augmentation strategy (DPMC) and a baseline version without this strategy (DPMC'). For comparison under diverse conditions, we employ datasets characterized by different markup percentages (w)

and proportions of discriminatory pricing (m), each comprising 100,000 orders to maintain evaluation consistency.

All experiments employ a uniform order information encoding method and the F1-score as the performance metric, with further details provided in the appendices section.

Comparative results are displayed in Table 4.2, showcasing the superior performance of our DPMC framework over other methods, including statistical-based HBOS [10], clustering-based CBLOF [11], distance-based KNN [12], angle-based ABOD [13], isolation-based IForest [14], density-based LOF [15], and probability-based ECOD [16] across various settings of w and m. The performance curves depicted in Fig. 4.4a and b illustrate F1-scores with respect to m at $w = 5\%$, and w at $m = 5\%$, respectively. These figures demonstrate that all anomaly detection methods struggle with this discriminatory pricing detection task, especially at lower w or m values where discriminatory pricing is more difficult to detect. However, our baseline method DPMC' outperforms these anomaly detection methods by a notable margin, and the introduction of the pseudo-pricing augmentation strategy significantly enhances performance, achieving high F1-scores even in challenging scenarios with small w or m.

Additionally, Fig. 4.4c-f illustrate boxplots of F1-scores across discriminatory pricing proportions m ranging from 1% to 30%, for markup percentages w of 5%, 10%, 15%, and 20%. While DPMC' surpasses other anomaly detection methods, its F1-scores exhibit considerable variability and do not consistently reach high levels. Conversely, DPMC, enhanced by the pseudo-pricing augmentation strategy, demonstrates both high performance and low variance in F1-scores, highlighting the effectiveness and robustness of our approach.

Our method operates in an unsupervised manner and does not require labels indicating discriminatory pricing. In Table 4.3, we further compare our method with supervised classification methods that utilize such labels. Specifically, for each order dataset of a particular w and m configuration, we construct an additional set of 100,000 order data following the same configuration, with explicitly prepared labels indicating whether each order involves discriminatory pricing. We use these labeled data as a training set for the supervised models, and then apply the trained model to the original order dataset for evaluation. Although the supervised methods have access to additional labeled data, our unsupervised DPMC approach outperforms them for most w and m configurations, especially in challenging cases where w and m are small. This superior performance can be attributed to our method's direct modeling of pricing strategies, which proves to be more effective for identifying discriminatory practices than straightforward supervised classification. These experimental results underscore the key advantages of our DPMC method: (1) DPMC removes the need for labeled training data, improving its practical applicability in real-world scenarios where such data may not be readily available; (2) Our method's ability to model pricing strategies directly from order data significantly enhances its generalization ability, making it more effective in adapting to and identifying discriminatory pricing in unknown scenarios.

Table 4.2 Comparative performance in discriminatory pricing detection

w	*m*	F1-score								
		Our models		Other models						
		DPMC	DPMC’	ABOD	CBLOF	HBOS	IForet	KNN	LOF	ECOD
5	1	**0.385**	0.030	0.008	0.005	0.007	0.008	0.008	0.002	0.005
	2	**0.542**	0.069	0.020	0.025	0.015	0.021	0.016	0.015	0.016
	3	**0.652**	0.112	0.031	0.034	0.024	0.029	0.024	0.026	0.021
	4	**0.703**	0.177	0.044	0.045	0.035	0.041	0.035	0.036	0.030
	5	**0.751**	0.240	0.054	0.057	0.045	0.050	0.042	0.047	0.040
	10	**0.842**	0.494	0.110	0.114	0.097	0.099	0.092	0.102	0.085
	15	**0.868**	0.662	0.166	0.164	0.150	0.154	0.141	0.155	0.131
	20	**0.888**	0.753	0.216	0.208	0.202	0.202	0.186	0.200	0.187
	30	**0.889**	0.844	0.315	0.304	0.304	0.304	0.277	0.297	0.269
10	1	**0.574**	0.035	0.015	0.017	0.010	0.009	0.013	0.011	0.006
	2	**0.721**	0.083	0.027	0.029	0.024	0.015	0.021	0.016	0.016
	3	**0.783**	0.142	0.044	0.042	0.033	0.026	0.028	0.026	0.027
	4	**0.829**	0.217	0.060	0.055	0.040	0.037	0.040	0.041	0.039
	5	**0.860**	0.304	0.069	0.069	0.049	0.048	0.049	0.049	0.047
	10	**0.917**	0.612	0.123	0.123	0.103	0.100	0.096	0.101	0.088
	15	**0.929**	0.772	0.174	0.178	0.158	0.154	0.144	0.153	0.133
	20	**0.934**	0.848	0.231	0.224	0.205	0.204	0.190	0.203	0.184
	30	**0.926**	0.922	0.326	0.314	0.306	0.303	0.280	0.300	0.277
15	1	**0.728**	0.035	0.022	0.014	0.012	0.009	0.015	0.016	0.009
	2	**0.824**	0.091	0.036	0.035	0.021	0.019	0.024	0.025	0.020
	3	**0.870**	0.180	0.046	0.052	0.029	0.025	0.029	0.034	0.027
	4	**0.899**	0.277	0.065	0.064	0.043	0.039	0.045	0.045	0.036
	5	**0.913**	0.413	0.082	0.079	0.053	0.052	0.058	0.055	0.046
	10	**0.941**	0.724	0.145	0.134	0.104	0.108	0.109	0.107	0.090
	15	**0.950**	0.855	0.200	0.186	0.154	0.160	0.156	0.158	0.135
	20	**0.950**	0.905	0.249	0.228	0.207	0.206	0.204	0.210	0.188
	30	0.946	**0.953**	0.337	0.319	0.312	0.309	0.291	0.309	0.272
20	1	**0.801**	0.038	0.032	0.020	0.012	0.009	0.019	0.016	0.011
	2	**0.887**	0.097	0.054	0.042	0.024	0.021	0.031	0.024	0.014
	3	**0.917**	0.216	0.070	0.060	0.032	0.032	0.045	0.035	0.027
	4	**0.934**	0.363	0.086	0.073	0.042	0.043	0.054	0.044	0.036
	5	**0.940**	0.487	0.100	0.084	0.050	0.055	0.065	0.052	0.045
	10	**0.958**	0.828	0.170	0.148	0.106	0.105	0.112	0.109	0.088
	15	**0.970**	0.902	0.218	0.199	0.159	0.156	0.164	0.165	0.143
	20	**0.970**	0.939	0.266	0.248	0.209	0.204	0.210	0.218	0.188
	30	0.951	**0.971**	0.352	0.325	0.311	0.313	0.299	0.313	0.282

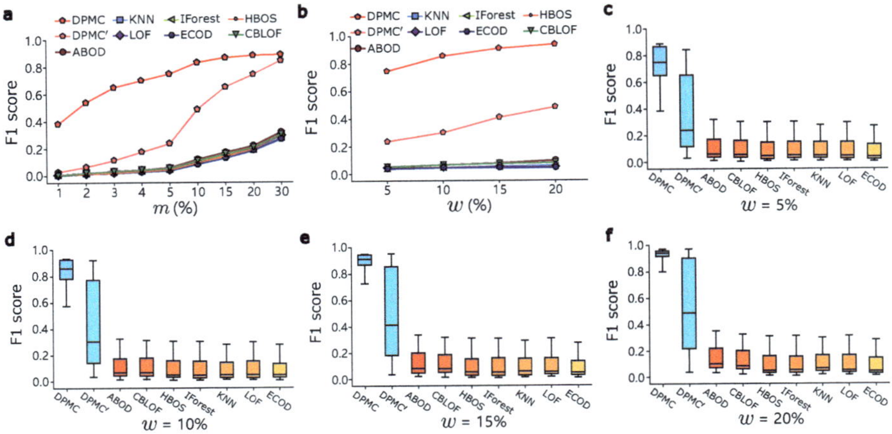

Fig. 4.4 Quantitative Results

4.2.5.2 Effect of Pricing Model Designs

To investigate the effects of different pricing model designs in our method, we utilize various regression models and evaluate their performance on an order dataset with $w = 10\%$ and $m = 10\%$. Table 4.4 presents the Mean Squared Error (MSE) of pricing prediction for these regression models, alongside their corresponding F1-scores in discriminatory pricing detection. These results demonstrate that lower MSE values correlate with higher F1-scores, suggesting that more accurate pricing models enhance the DPMC's ability to accurately distinguish orders.

Figure 4.5a-e include scatter plots that compare actual and predicted prices, providing a visual representation of the pricing prediction accuracy of different models. Notably, the decision tree (DT) model achieves the most accurate pricing prediction and the highest F1-score for discriminatory pricing detection. Furthermore, the accuracy of the markup percentage w^* estimation in our pseudo-pricing augmentation strategy is also influenced by the efficacy of the pricing model. Figure 4.5a-e show the density curves modeled for w^* estimation by different pricing models using Kernel Density Estimation (detailed in the pseudo-pricing augmentation for DPMC section). The DT model provides the most precise estimation, with an estimated $w^* = 0.1013$ closely matching the actual dataset markup percentage of $w = 10\%$. Poorer performing models, depicted in Fig. 4.5d-e, fail to estimate w^*. Given these results, the DT regression model is chosen as the default pricing model within our DPMC framework. Additionally, Fig. 4.5f highlights the top five important features impacting pricing model performance: trip distance, vehicle type, nighttime, weather conditions, and the number of passengers (carpooling status), which align closely with their importance in actual pricing. These analysis results emphasize the importance of selecting an appropriate pricing model for the DPMC framework, which is fundamental to ensuring its accuracy and reliability in detecting discriminatory pricing.

Table 4.3 Comparative performance in discriminatory pricing detection

w(%)	m(%)	F1-score				
		Unspervised		Supervised		
		DPMC	DPMC'	DT [17]	GB [18]	POLY [19]
	1	**0.385**	0.030	0.008	0.009	0.000
	2	**0.542**	0.069	0.039	0.025	0.000
	3	**0.652**	0.112	0.063	0.031	0.000
	4	**0.703**	0.177	0.081	0.033	0.000
5	5	**0.751**	0.240	0.257	0.046	0.101
	10	**0.842**	0.494	0.533	0.198	0.401
	15	**0.868**	0.662	0.627	0.384	0.538
	20	**0.888**	0.753	0.688	0.524	0.628
	30	**0.889**	0.844	0.758	0.695	0.722
	1	**0.574**	0.035	0.080	0.044	0.032
	2	**0.721**	0.083	0.247	0.182	0.264
	3	**0.783**	0.142	0.332	0.268	0.418
	4	**0.829**	0.217	0.402	0.296	0.505
10	5	**0.860**	0.304	0.458	0.414	0.550
	10	**0.917**	0.612	0.717	0.666	0.661
	15	**0.929**	0.772	0.799	0.797	0.703
	20	**0.934**	0.848	0.850	0.844	0.734
	30	**0.926**	0.922	0.889	0.920	0.791
	1	**0.728**	0.035	0.213	0.136	0.272
	2	**0.824**	0.091	0.332	0.347	0.528
	3	**0.870**	0.180	0.506	0.469	0.608
	4	**0.899**	0.277	0.635	0.572	0.651
15	5	**0.913**	0.413	0.685	0.654	0.672
	10	**0.941**	0.724	0.816	0.845	0.720
	15	**0.950**	0.855	0.872	0.915	0.746
	20	0.950	0.905	0.901	**0.950**	0.769
	30	0.946	0.953	0.932	**0.976**	0.815
	1	**0.801**	0.038	0.314	0.313	0.470
	2	**0.887**	0.097	0.508	0.556	0.604
	3	**0.917**	0.216	0.650	0.671	0.656
	4	**0.934**	0.363	0.729	0.739	0.687
20	5	**0.940**	0.487	0.767	0.809	0.706
	10	**0.958**	0.828	0.874	0.932	0.745
	15	**0.970**	0.902	0.914	0.967	0.765
	20	0.970	0.939	0.932	**0.978**	0.787
	30	0.951	0.971	0.947	**0.989**	0.832

Table 4.4 Relationship between predictive performance of pricing models and F1-scores

Model	MSE	F1-score
DT regression [20]	33.951	0.908
GB regression [21]	98.363	0.810
Poly regression [22]	208.545	0.517
KNN regression [23]	2965.447	0.209
Linear regression [24]	7946.057	0.162

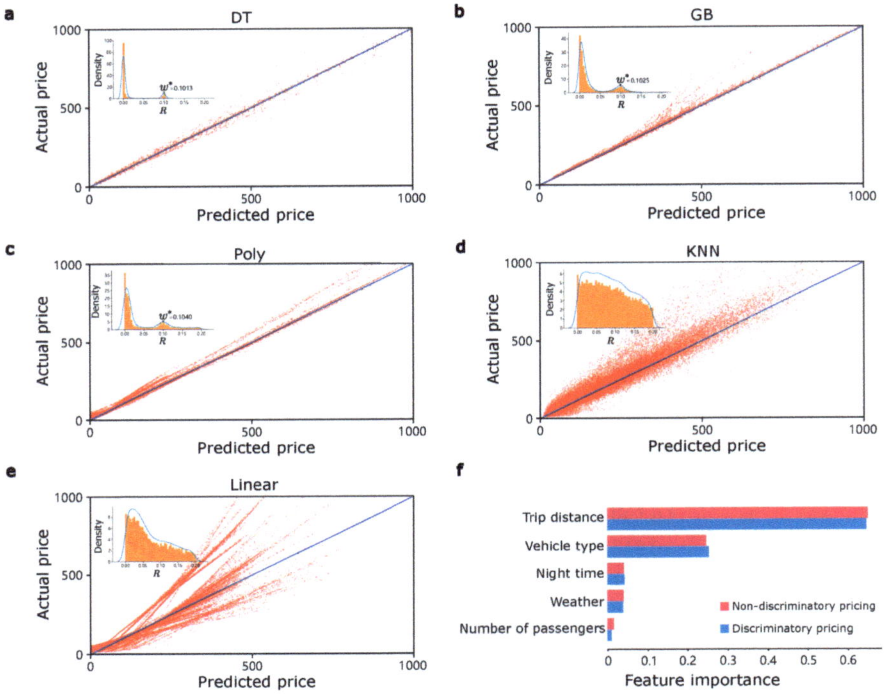

Fig. 4.5 Analysis of pricing model performance

4.2.5.3 Effect of Pseudo-Pricing Augmentation Strategy

In our method, the pseudo-pricing augmentation strategy, as depicted in Fig. 4.6a and detailed in the methods section, is proposed to address the data imbalance problem between discriminatory/non-discriminatory pricing orders within the ride-hailing order dataset. Such imbalance can severely degrade model performance, especially when the proportion of discriminatory pricing orders is low. For instance, as illustrated in Fig. 4.6b, when the proportion of discriminatory pricing orders (m) decreases from 30% to 10%, there is a notable increase in pricing prediction errors for both discriminatory ($E_d^{'}$) and non-discriminatory ($E_{nd}^{'}$) pricing models, which

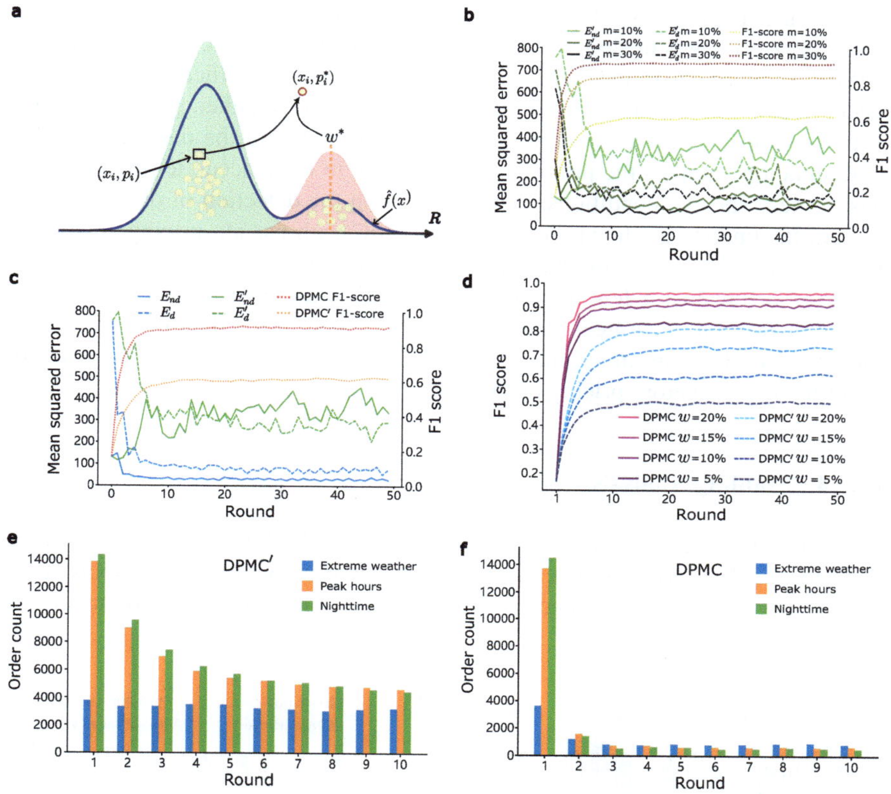

Fig. 4.6 Effect of pseudo-pricing augmentation analysis

consequently leads to a significant decline in the F1-score for discriminatory pricing detection.

Figure 4.6c showcases the performance curves of pricing prediction and discriminatory pricing detection over learning rounds for both DMPC' (without pseudo-pricing augmentation) and DPMC (with pseudo-pricing augmentation). After implementing the pseudo-pricing augmentation strategy, there is a noticeable improvement in prediction accuracy for both discriminatory and non-discriminatory pricing models, as evidenced by the rapidly converging MSE values (E_d and E_{nd}). This enhancement directly contributes to a significant performance boost in discriminatory pricing detection, as indicated by the curve of "DPMC F1-score". Moreover, the F1-score curves in Fig. 4.6d across different markup percentages ($w = 5\%, 10\%, 15\%, 20\%$) demonstrate that DPMC not only converges faster but also achieves better performance than DPMC', underscoring the effectiveness of the pseudo-pricing strategy in alleviating data imbalance and enhancing detection capabilities.

To further explore how the pseudo-pricing augmentation strategy improves discriminatory pricing detection, we analyze the information of misclassified orders by DPMC' over learning rounds. As depicted in Fig. 4.6e, misclassifications by DPMC' predominantly occur under conditions such as extreme weather, peak hours, and nighttime—scenarios that are typically underrepresented in the data. This underrepresentation hampers the pricing model's ability to learn accurate pricing strategies in these specific conditions, thereby affecting the detection of discriminatory pricing. In contrast, as shown in Fig. 4.6f, DPMC with pseudo-pricing augmentation significantly reduces the number of misclassified orders in these challenging scenarios within just a few learning rounds. This demonstrates that the pseudo-pricing augmentation strategy can effectively augment order data to facilitate the pricing model learning in special scenarios, ultimately enhancing the accuracy of detecting discriminatory pricing behaviors.

4.2.5.4 Stability Analysis

Figure 4.7 illustrates the detection performance of the DPMC model under specific scenarios, such as trip distance and extreme weather conditions. We thoroughly evaluate the model's performance across various distance ranges (a), vehicle types

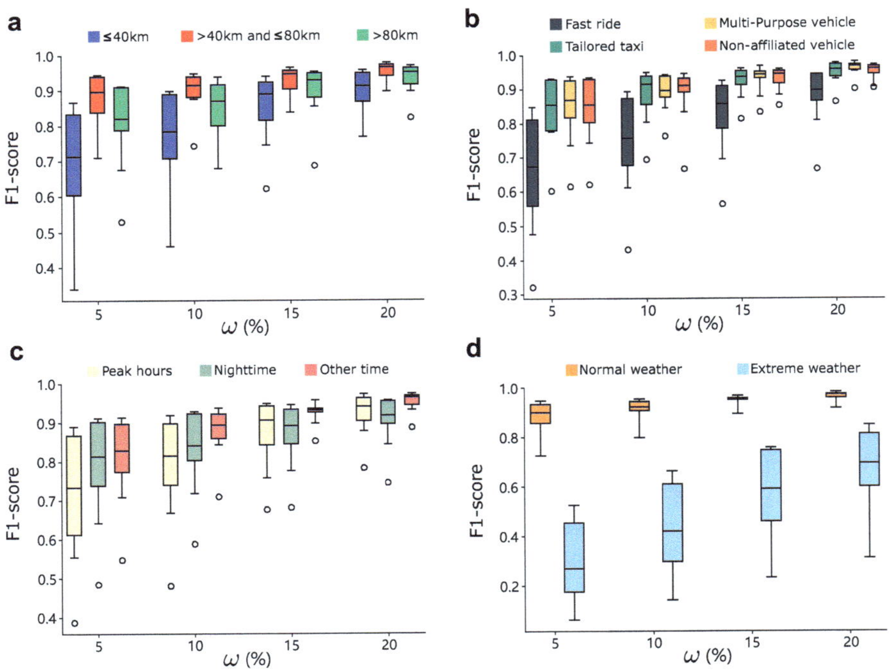

Fig. 4.7 Performance of the DPMC model in specific scenarios

(b), time periods (c), and weather conditions (d). In the dataset, the price markup ratio (w) ranges from 5% to 20%, with corresponding discriminatory pricing ratios (m) of 1%, 2%, 3%, 4%, 5%, 10%, 15%, 20%, and 30%. The box plot analysis reveals that our method demonstrates high stability across different scenarios. The box plots clearly show the distribution of prediction errors for the DPMC model under various conditions, with most scenarios exhibiting small error ranges, indicating that the model is robust to a wide variety of interfering factors. Furthermore, as shown by the box plot results, our approach consistently exhibits high stability across different conditions, with the majority of prediction errors remaining within a narrow range, suggesting the model's strong resilience to diverse types of disturbances.

4.2.6 Discussion

This study presents an in-depth analysis of our proposed Dual Pricing Model Clustering (DPMC) framework, highlighting its innovative approach to detecting discriminatory pricing within the ride-hailing industry. Our unsupervised clustering algorithm demonstrates three key characteristics that enhance its effectiveness: insensitivity to currency systems, adaptability to various platform pricing strategies, and significant scalability. These features make the algorithm highly versatile, allowing it to process data across different currencies and adapt to diverse pricing strategies while maintaining scalability across various industries.

4.2.6.1 Insensitivity to Currency Systems

In the context of antitrust monitoring and the detection of discriminatory pricing, a crucial consideration is the insensitivity of the proposed Dual Pricing Model Clustering (DPMC) framework to variations in currency systems. This characteristic is pivotal for the model's generalizability across different geographic regions and markets. Discriminatory pricing practices often transcend local currency distinctions, particularly within global platform economies where transactions occur in multiple currencies. The DPMC framework's reliance on relative price differences rather than absolute currency values ensures that it remains robust and effective across diverse currency environments. This insensitivity is achieved through the framework's foundational reliance on the price prediction differentials between discriminatory and non-discriminatory pricing models. Since the framework operates on the principle of identifying patterns in pricing behavior rather than focusing on absolute price values, it is inherently designed to function effectively regardless of the currency in which the transactions are conducted. This adaptability is further reinforced by the pseudo-pricing augmentation strategy, which normalizes pricing data across different scales, thereby enhancing the model's ability to detect discriminatory pricing in varied currency contexts.

4.2.6.2 Adaptability to Platform Pricing Strategies

In the context of an ever-evolving platform economy, adaptability to diverse and dynamic pricing strategies is critical for any antitrust monitoring framework. Our proposed DPMC framework's robustness stems from its iterative learning mechanism, which allows it to adapt dynamically to various platform pricing strategies that are often opaque and change rapidly. The cyclical "model learning → data clustering" process employed by DPMC enables the framework to continuously refine its understanding of both discriminatory and non-discriminatory pricing strategies as they evolve. This adaptability is essential, particularly in the ride-hailing sector, where platforms frequently adjust their pricing algorithms in response to market conditions, consumer demand, and regulatory pressures.

The integration of a pseudo-pricing augmentation strategy further enhances the adaptability of DPMC. By generating synthetic data that reflects possible discriminatory pricing scenarios, this strategy allows the framework to maintain high detection accuracy even when faced with new or uncommon pricing strategies. As a result, DPMC is not only capable of identifying existing discriminatory pricing practices but is also well-equipped to detect emerging strategies that have not yet been widely adopted.

4.2.6.3 Scalability

The scalability of the DPMC framework is crucial for its application across various platform economies, extending beyond the ride-hailing industry to fields such as food delivery and travel services. These industries generate vast amounts of order data, with pricing influenced by factors such as delivery distance, weather, and traffic congestion. The DPMC framework is designed to efficiently scale with these large datasets, employing iterative model learning and data clustering processes to uncover different pricing patterns and detect discriminatory pricing behaviors by identifying hidden pricing models within the orders. Additionally, the introduction of the pseudo-pricing enhancement strategy effectively mitigates sample imbalance, further enhancing the framework's adaptability to different data environments. This scalability makes the DPMC framework a versatile tool for antitrust monitoring across multiple platform industries, ensuring that fair pricing practices are maintained as these markets evolve and develop.

In conclusion, the DPMC framework represents a comprehensive approach to detecting discriminatory pricing, characterized by its insensitivity to currency systems, adaptability to dynamic pricing strategies, and scalability across industries. Our experimental results underscore the framework's superior performance compared to existing mainstream anomaly detection algorithms, affirming its potential to drive meaningful improvements in market oversight and regulatory practices. By applying the DPMC framework across various service platforms, we can promote fair pricing behavior and enhance antitrust monitoring, contributing to the maintenance of equitable market dynamics across industries.

4.3 Chapter Summary

This chapter provides an in-depth exploration of the economic principles of price discrimination, its relationship with antitrust issues, and the regulatory challenges involved. By introducing a dual pricing model clustering framework, we developed a method for identifying discriminatory pricing behaviors from a machine learning perspective. Additionally, we demonstrated the process of dataset construction and detection in the context of ride-hailing platforms. The experimental results in this chapter indicate that the dual pricing model clustering-based discriminatory pricing detection framework excels in handling complex scenarios and data imbalances, offering strong stability, adaptability, and scalability. The pseudo-pricing augmentation strategy further enhances the model's detection performance, enabling the Dual Pricing Model Clustering (DPMC) to effectively accommodate various pricing strategies and different monetary systems, showcasing its broad potential for application in antitrust monitoring.

Chapter 5
Intelligent System Framework for Computational Antitrust: Risk Modeling, Large-Model Integration, and Functional Demonstration

Abstract This chapter presents a comprehensive framework for the design and implementation of an intelligent system for computational antitrust, focusing on risk modeling, large model integration, and functional demonstration. It begins with an in-depth analysis of monopolistic behavior types observed in the platform economy, including monopoly agreements, concentrations of undertakings, and abuses of market dominance. Building upon this foundation, a three-tiered risk level system is constructed to classify monopolistic behaviors as low, medium, or high risk, supported by a detailed evaluation of ten key data elements such as market share, entry barriers, network effects, data control, and consumer welfare.

The chapter further proposes an intelligent antitrust system architecture that integrates machine learning, knowledge graphs, and large-scale language models to enable real time detection, risk prediction, and regulatory decision support. Through modular design, the system encompasses key functional components—data management, risk identification, visualization, compliance auditing, and intelligent report generation—ensuring adaptability and scalability for complex regulatory scenarios. A computational antitrust large model, fine-tuned using domain-specific corpora and integrated via APIs, provides advanced reasoning and natural language generation capabilities for automated report drafting and cross-departmental coordination.

Functional demonstrations highlight the system's ability to perform statistical analysis, identify discriminatory pricing through Dual Pricing Model Clustering (DPMC), predict monopoly risk trends, and generate intelligent risk assessment reports. The chapter concludes by emphasizing the transformative role of computational antitrust systems in modern governance—enhancing the scientific basis, efficiency, and intelligence of antitrust regulation in the era of the digital economy.

Keywords Computational antitrust · Intelligent risk assessment system · Monopolistic behavior · Platform economy · Risk level modeling · Data element analysis · Large language model integration · Knowledge graph · Machine learning · Regulatory decision support

W. Liu, *Computational Antitrust*, Artificial Intelligence and the Rule of Law,
https://doi.org/10.1007/978-981-95-5037-1_5

5.1 Design of Monopolistic Behavior Risk Assessment System

5.1.1 Analysis of Monopolistic Behavior Types

The monopolistic practices commonly observed among platform enterprises can be broadly categorized into three types: monopoly agreements, concentrations of undertakings, and abuse of market dominance. Among these, monopoly agreements refer to collusive arrangements—either formal or informal—between platform enterprises themselves or between platforms and the operators within them, with the intent to eliminate or restrict competition. These agreements may take the form of written contracts, oral understandings, or other coordinated actions. Such conduct manifests in various ways. For instance, platform enterprises may agree to fix the prices of certain goods or services, thereby depriving consumers of access to lower prices that would otherwise emerge in a competitive market. They may also impose restrictions on production or sales volumes, artificially creating shortages to inflate prices. Additionally, platform companies might engage in market allocation schemes to avoid direct competition and preserve their respective market positions.

These monopoly agreements severely impair market competition. They reduce the efficiency of resource allocation and deny consumers the benefits of vigorous market rivalry. Furthermore, such agreements can stifle technological innovation and hinder industrial upgrading, as firms lacking competitive pressure may also lack the incentive to innovate.

Operator concentration among platform enterprises, also referred to as merger and acquisition (M&A) activities, involves the consolidation of two or more platform firms or the acquisition—whether partial or complete—of control by one or more platform enterprises over others. Such concentration leads to lasting changes in the structure of inter-enterprise relationships. In practical terms, this includes corporate mergers, the acquisition of controlling stakes or assets, and the exercise of decisive influence over other operators through contractual or similar arrangements.

These concentration activities may yield dual effects. On one hand, they can generate economies of scale and enhance the competitive capacity of the firms involved. On the other hand, excessive concentration risks the reinforcement of market dominance, the restriction of fair competition, the erosion of market efficiency, and the emergence of monopolistic structures. These outcomes may ultimately compromise consumer welfare and broader public interests. Consequently, operator concentration among platform enterprises must be subject to rigorous legal scrutiny and regulatory oversight to strike a balance between promoting efficiency gains and preserving a competitive market structure. Such oversight is essential to safeguarding orderly market functioning and ensuring the integrity of competition.

The abuse of market dominance by platform enterprises—manifested in practices such as exclusive dealing, "pick one from two" policies, and other exclusionary behaviors—refers to a series of anti-competitive strategies employed by dominant platforms to exclude or restrict competition. Once a platform attains a position of market dominance, it may leverage its superior market position to engage in the following conduct:

Exclusive Dealing: This refers to the practice where a platform enterprise imposes trading restrictions on its counterparties, requiring them to transact exclusively with the platform itself or with designated partners. Such constraints limit the counterparties' freedom of choice. For instance, a platform may mandate that merchants sell their products or services solely through its own channels, prohibiting any sales on competing platforms.

Pick One from Two (Forced Exclusivity): This is a prototypical form of exclusionary conduct, wherein platform enterprises compel merchants to choose between rival platforms. Such coercion is often enforced through preferential access to resources, traffic support, or punitive measures. Merchants are pressured to abandon operations on competing platforms, thereby entrenching the dominant platform's monopoly position. This practice is particularly prevalent in the e-commerce sector, as exemplified by the Alibaba case, where the company was accused of implementing such policies to restrict competition.

Other Exclusionary Practices: Exclusionary conduct is a central concern in antitrust enforcement and takes on a variety of forms beyond the well-known "pick one from two" strategy. It includes entering into exclusive agreements, erecting technical barriers, and intentionally increasing entry thresholds, all with the goal of preserving the incumbent's dominant position and deterring potential challengers. These tactics undermine market diversity, reduce competition, and stifle innovation. Among these, algorithmic price discrimination based on big data, often referred to as "data-enabled price steering," has attracted particular scrutiny. In this practice, platforms analyze vast amounts of user data to implement personalized pricing schemes, wherein existing users—despite receiving identical goods or services—are charged higher prices compared to new or price-sensitive users. This form of discrimination infringes upon consumers' right to fair treatment and distorts market order, constituting a form of exploitative abuse.

These practices restrict the full play of market competition, making it difficult for other competitors to enter or operate effectively within the market, which in turn reduces overall market dynamism and efficiency. With competition curtailed, consumers may face reduced choices, higher prices, and declining service quality, thus harming their legitimate rights and interests. In the absence of competitive pressure, firms may also lose the incentive to innovate, thereby impairing the innovation capacity and technological progress of the entire industry. The abuse of market dominance disrupts the order of fair competition, posing a threat to the sound development of a market economy.

Given that platform enterprises vary significantly in their market influence, merely detecting monopolistic behaviors is insufficient for effective regulation. It is therefore essential to conduct risk assessments of suspected monopolistic conduct by platform firms, enabling early intervention and proactive prevention of anticompetitive practices.

5.1.2 Construction of Risk Levels for Antitrust Behavior

The construction of a risk level system for monopolistic behavior is a complex and systematic task that requires comprehensive consideration of various factors and dimensions, including market concentration, entry barriers, market conduct diversity, and the impact on consumer welfare. Academic research on monopolistic behavior mainly draws from economics, law, and management, analyzing the characteristics and harms of monopolistic behavior in different domains. In antitrust enforcement, authorities must scientifically assess the nature and risk level of monopolistic behavior based on specific case circumstances, considering market structure, conduct, and its resulting market effects. Currently, there is no unified method for evaluating the risk levels of monopolistic behavior in academic research, and both theoretical and practical explorations in different countries are continuously enriching the knowledge system in this field.

To develop an effective risk classification assessment method, this study draws on risk assessment methods from other fields, such as the risk evaluation of equipment failures [1] and risk classification methods in the financial industry [2]. Some literature defines risk levels using a quantitative scoring system. For example, a score between 80 and 100 is classified as low risk, while a score between 0 and 50 is considered high risk [3]. Furthermore, in the study of regional financial risk early warning systems, risk levels are categorized as high, medium, and low risk [4], aiming to quantify the degree of risk and guide corresponding mitigation measures. These classification methods shift from subjective assessments to standardized, quantitative approaches, making risk evaluation more scientific and objective.

Based on this, this study proposes a three-tiered risk level system for monopolistic behavior in the digital economy: low risk, medium risk, and high risk, in order to effectively communicate the level of risk and urgency.

Low Risk Level: Low-risk monopolistic behavior refers to situations where platform companies apply big data technologies in their pricing strategies but do not significantly negatively impact market competition or consumer welfare. For example, platforms may reasonably use user data for personalized recommendations or price optimization. While such behavior is differentiated, it does not deviate from the basic principles of market competition. Although these actions may seem to have no obvious harm to competition or consumer welfare, over the long term, they could hinder the market entry of new players, thus impacting market diversity and competitive intensity. Such low-risk behavior generally stays within the bounds of reasonable competition, but without proper attention, it may gradually accumulate negative effects on market order.

Medium Risk Level: Medium-risk behavior primarily includes platforms leveraging big data technology for some level of differentiated pricing, such as "big data price discrimination." In such cases, consumers are charged different prices based on their consumption habits or browsing history, leading to unreasonably high prices for certain consumer groups. While this differentiated pricing may not disrupt the market as a whole, it can result in unfair treatment for some consumers, thereby raising concerns and the possibility of regulatory intervention. The existence of such practices undermines market transparency and consumer trust, especially when platform companies hold significant market share.

High Risk Level: High-risk monopolistic behavior is characterized by strong exclusivity and destructiveness, often involving tactics such as restrictive agreements, market blocking, and tie-ins to exclude competitors or limit market entry. For example, platforms may use their dominant market position to sign exclusive agreements, force entry barriers, or manipulate prices through data manipulation, directly harming market fairness and efficiency. These actions reduce market competition and have a direct negative impact on consumer welfare. High-risk monopolistic behavior can also enable platforms to control prices and quality, forcing consumers to pay above reasonable levels, ultimately impairing the healthy development of the market.

In conclusion, this three-tiered risk level system is designed to provide a clear framework for evaluating monopolistic behavior in the digital economy. It aims to help identify the characteristics of risks and balance their potential impacts more scientifically. The next step will involve further analyzing various data elements in the market to build a scientifically sound and reasonable risk assessment model.

5.1.3 Analysis of the Data Elements for Monopolistic Behavior Risk Levels

Compared to traditional industries, the platform economy sector in China is characterized by high market concentration, substantial entry barriers, and information opacity, among other prominent features. These factors make it easier for platform companies to dominate the market and establish monopolistic structures. However, there is currently a lack of universally recognized and quantifiable standards for determining monopolistic behavior in platform companies. Existing academic research typically analyzes and assesses the causes and severity of monopolistic behavior from three dimensions: market structure, market conduct, and market impact. Therefore, this study synthesizes and refines ten key characteristics from these three perspectives, which are of significant reference value for assessing the risk levels of monopolistic behavior. These characteristics include: market share, market concentration, entry barriers, customer dependency, price control ability, network effects, data control and processing capabilities, competitor behavior, consumer welfare impact, and the regulatory environment.

Based on these characteristics, we further refine and quantify the relevant data elements to construct an evaluation system capable of comprehensively reflecting the monopolistic behavior risk level of platform companies when utilizing big data technologies for pricing. This system not only provides a quantifiable basis for assessing monopolistic behavior risks but also serves as a reference for early warning and regulatory decision-making.

It is important to note that the quantification ranges in Table 5.1 are based on general assumptions. In practical applications, they should be adjusted to suit specific industries and market environments. Furthermore, for certain subjective features (such as customer dependency and network effects), quantitative assessments often require a comprehensive analysis of market research, user feedback, and other data sources. Next, we will conduct a detailed data element-level quantitative analysis of these features.

Market share, also known as market penetration, refers to the proportion of sales (or revenue) that a company holds in the market for a particular product, especially when compared to its competitors. The higher the market share of a platform enterprise, the greater the potential risk to the market when the company is suspected of monopolistic behavior. Market concentration, on the other hand, refers to the proportion of market share held by the few largest firms in a given market, often referred to as "leading" or "dominant" firms. This index is typically calculated by summing the market shares of the few largest firms. The larger the combined market share of the leading firms, the higher the market concentration. In our research, we use the Herfindahl-Hirschman Index (HHI) to specifically measure industry market concentration. The HHI value ranges from 0 to 1. A larger HHI indicates higher market concentration, a higher degree of monopoly, and consequently greater potential risk.

Table 5.1 Digital features for monopolistic risk level assessment

Digital feature	Feature explanation	Examples
Market Share	The share of the platform in the relevant market, reflecting the platform's market dominance and control.	High: Market share exceeds 20%Medium: Market share between 10%–20%Low: Market share below 10%
Market Concentration (HHI)	The degree of market competition, measured by the Herfindahl-Hirschman Index (HHI). The higher the value, the higher the market concentration and monopolistic risk.	High: $0.7 \leq HHI < 1$Medium: $0.4 \leq HHI < 0.7$Low: $0 \leq HHI < 0.4$
Entry Barriers	The ease with which new competitors can enter the market. High entry barriers may protect incumbent companies' market positions.	Extremely high entry costs or regulatory restrictions indicate high risk; moderate barriers indicate medium risk; low barriers or easy market entry indicate low risk.
Customer Dependency	The degree to which consumers rely on the platform. High dependency may indicate strong bargaining power and market control.	High risk: Consumers heavily rely on a single platform. Medium risk: Moderate dependency with alternative options. Low risk: Low dependency with multiple alternatives.
Price Control Ability	The platform's ability to control or significantly influence prices. Independent pricing power is a hallmark of market dominance.	High risk: Platform can unilaterally decide prices. Medium risk: Platform has some influence on prices. Low risk: Prices are significantly affected by market competition.

(continued)

Table 5.1 (continued)

Digital feature	Feature explanation	Examples
Network Effects	The strength of the platform's network effects. Strong network effects can lead to a "winner-takes-all" market structure, increasing monopolistic risk.	High risk: Extremely strong network effects, difficult to break. Medium risk: Noticeable network effects, but competition exists. Low risk: Limited network effects.
Data Control and Processing Capability	The platform's ability to control and process data, especially in using big data for market analysis and decision-making. Data advantages can enhance the platform's market position.	High risk: Platform has absolute control over critical data. Medium risk: Platform has some data control. Low risk: Platform has limited control over data.
Competitor Behavior	The number and strength of competitors and their market conduct. The number and strength of competitors directly impact market competition.	High risk: Few or no competitors, unable to compete effectively. Medium risk: Some effective competitors. Low risk: Multiple strong competitors.
Consumer Welfare Impact	The impact of platform behavior on consumer welfare, including factors like price, choice, and service quality. Monopolistic behavior may harm consumer welfare.	High risk: Limited consumer choice, high prices, low innovation. Medium risk: Moderate impact on choice and price. Low risk: Minimal impact on consumer welfare.
Regulatory Environment	The regulatory environment of the relevant market, including the rigor and enforcement of laws and regulations. Effective regulation can reduce monopolistic behavior.	High risk: Lax regulation, lack of effective constraints on monopolistic behavior. Medium risk: Some regulation, but enforcement is weak. Low risk: Strict regulation and effective enforcement.

In a perfectly monopolistic market, the HHI is equal to 1. In contrast, in a market with many firms of equal size, the HHI approaches 0 (Table 5.2).

Barriers to entry refer to the various obstacles and constraints that new entrants face when attempting to enter a market or industry. These barriers impact the freedom of market competition and the likelihood of new competitors entering, thereby strengthening the market position of existing firms and potentially leading to market monopolization. To comprehensively assess barriers to entry in an industry, it is essential to identify and quantify key data elements. Based on the analysis of market competition structures, we consider the following six categories of factors as essential data elements for evaluating technological barriers:

Capital Requirements: Capital requirements measure the initial investment needed to enter an industry. High capital demands restrict the entry capabilities of potential entrants, particularly in areas such as R&D investment and production facility construction. By evaluating capital intensity and fixed asset investments, the strength of capital barriers can be quantified.

Table 5.2 Analysis of data elements related to barriers to entry

Data element	Explanation	Quantification example
Capital requirements	Assess the initial investment required to enter a particular market or industry. High capital requirements (such as expensive equipment or significant startup funds) create significant entry barriers.	Example of startup capital estimates: High risk: Over $10 million Medium risk: Between $1 million and $10 million Low risk: Less than $1 million
Technological barriers	Assess the level of technical knowledge and expertise required to enter the market. High technological barriers imply significant R&D investments or specialized knowledge. Qualitative analysis: Study the technical complexity within the industry, distribution of patents, and intellectual property.	High risk: R&D investment exceeds 15% of revenue. Medium risk: 5% to 15% of revenue. Low risk: Less than 5%.
Economies of scale	Assess whether existing firms gain cost advantages due to their scale, with larger production volumes reducing unit costs and creating barriers for new entrants. Qualitative analysis: Examine the scale and market share of leading firms in the industry and evaluate how economies of scale affect new entrants.	High risk: Unit cost decreases by more than 30% with increased production scale. Medium risk: Unit cost decreases by 10% to 30%. Low risk: Unit cost decreases by less than 10%.
Regulations and policies	Assess the time and cost of obtaining the necessary licenses. Strict regulations or high licensing thresholds can serve as barriers to entry. Qualitative analysis: Analyze relevant laws, industry standards, and their potential impact on new firms.	High risk: License acquisition takes more than 12 months and costs more than $500,000. Medium risk: 3 to 12 months and costs between $100,000 and $500,000. Low risk: Less than 3 months and costs less than $100,000.
Brand loyalty and customer retention	Assess consumer loyalty to existing brands. Strong brand loyalty and customer retention make it difficult for new entrants to attract customers. Qualitative analysis: Investigate consumer awareness of and preference for existing brands, as well as the potential costs and likelihood of brand switching.	High risk: Customer switching costs exceed 50% of the average product or service price. Medium risk: Switching costs range between 10% and 50%. Low risk: Switching costs are less than 10%.
Channel control	Assess the extent to which existing firms control key distribution channels, as this can limit new entrants' market exposure. Qualitative analysis: Examine the position of existing firms in the supply chain and distribution networks and their potential to obstruct new entrants.	High risk: 1–2 firms control over 70% of distribution channels. Medium risk: 3–5 firms control between 40% and 70% of distribution channels. Low risk: More than 5 firms, none of which control more than 40% of the distribution channels.

Technological Barriers: Technological barriers refer to the competitive advantage that firms hold in key technologies, which are often difficult to replicate or master in the short term. Indicators such as the number of patents, the ratio of R&D expenditure, and the maturity of technologies can quantify the level of technological barriers, reflecting the technical thresholds for industry entry.

Economies of Scale: Economies of scale refer to the effects whereby firms reduce unit costs as production scales up. Firms with significant economies of scale tend to have lower marginal costs, making it difficult for new entrants to compete. Analyzing market concentration and the cost structure of firms helps evaluate the existence and impact of economies of scale barriers.

Regulations and Policies: Regulatory and policy barriers arise from industry oversight, legal restrictions, or government licensing requirements. The level of regulatory strictness in different markets can significantly affect the difficulty of entry. Therefore, analyzing industry entry permits and regulatory requirements is essential to quantifying the strength of regulatory barriers.

Brand Loyalty and Customer Retention: Brand loyalty and customer retention significantly increase barriers to entry, as new entrants struggle to quickly gain the trust of existing customers. By analyzing market research data, customer satisfaction levels, and brand market share, the impact of brand barriers can be quantified.

Channel Control: Channel control barriers arise from existing firms' dominance over distribution channels, making it difficult for new entrants to gain market share. Data such as distribution coverage, depth of the distribution network, and investment in sales networks can be used to assess the existence and strength of channel barriers.

In conclusion, these six categories of data elements provide a systematic framework for evaluating barriers to entry. Through comprehensive analysis of these factors, the competitive structure of an industry and the potential risks of monopolization can be revealed.

Customer dependency refers to the extent to which customers rely on a specific platform, product, or service. It reflects how well a business meets customer demands and the stickiness of the relationship between customers and the business. Customer dependency is a key indicator for evaluating whether a business possesses technological barriers, as a high degree of customer dependency typically leads to lower customer mobility, thereby strengthening the company's market control and competitive barriers.

To systematically assess customer dependency, this monograph proposes five categories of data elements as the foundation for building such an evaluation (Table 5.3):

Availability of Substitutes or Services: If there are few alternative products or services in the market, customers tend to be more dependent on the existing platform. This data element assesses the quantity and quality of similar products in the market, analyzing the scope of customer substitution options. It indirectly reflects the strength of a company's technological barriers.

Table 5.3 Analysis of customer dependency-related data elements

Data element	Explanation	Quantitative example
Availability of substitutes or services	A critical indicator for assessing market structure and competitive dynamics, this measures the extent to which customers rely on a specific platform or supplier's products or services.	**High risk:** Few or no substitutes are available, e.g., fewer than 10% of customers can find suitable alternatives. **Medium risk:** Some substitutes are available, with approximately 30%–60% of customers finding suitable alternatives. **Low risk:** Substitutes are widely available, and more than 70% of customers can find suitable alternatives.
Customer spending proportion on a specific platform	The proportion of a customer's overall expenditure allocated to a specific platform or supplier. This indicator reflects the customer's degree of reliance on the platform. A higher spending ratio implies greater reliance, which often results in higher switching costs and lower likelihood of substitution.	**High risk:** Customer spending on the platform accounts for over 70% of their total relevant expenditure. **Medium risk:** Spending proportion is between 40%–70%. **Low risk:** Spending proportion is less than 40%.
Customer retention rate	This measures the proportion of customers retained by a business over a specific period, serving as a key indicator of customer loyalty and product/service stickiness. A high retention rate typically indicates strong customer satisfaction and dependency, suggesting that the business enjoys a competitive advantage in maintaining customer relationships.	**High risk:** Annual retention rate exceeds 90%. **Medium risk:** Annual retention rate is between 70%–90%. **Low risk:** Annual retention rate is below 70%.
Customer switching costs	The various costs customers incur when transitioning from their current platform or supplier to alternative products or services. These costs include not only direct economic expenditures but also hidden costs such as time, effort, and risks, which often significantly influence customer decision-making and behavior.	**High risk:** Switching costs exceed 50% of the customer's annual expenditure on the platform. **Medium risk:** Switching costs range from 25%–50%. **Low risk:** Switching costs are less than 25%.
Impact of single supplier on customer business	In antitrust analysis, when a customer's critical business processes heavily depend on a single supplier, the customer faces higher switching costs and business disruption risks, thus diminishing their options.	**High risk:** Business impact exceeds 50% if the customer stops using the supplier. **Medium risk:** Impact is between 20%–50%. **Low risk:** Impact is less than 20%.

Customer Spending Proportion on a Specific Platform: The higher the proportion of a customer's total spending on a specific platform, the stronger the customer's dependency on that platform. This metric quantifies the importance of the platform's products or services to the customer and serves as a crucial reference for assessing customer loyalty and market dependency.

Customer Retention Rate: This metric measures the percentage of customers who continue using the platform's products or services within a given timeframe. A high retention rate indicates ongoing customer dependency, and it is a significant data point for assessing both customer reliance and the business's market barriers.

Customer Switching Costs: Switching costs refer to the time, money, and effort a customer must invest to move from the current platform to an alternative one. The higher the switching costs, the greater the dependency, as customers tend to stay on the current platform to avoid these costs. Analyzing switching costs provides valuable insights into identifying a company's competitive barriers.

Impact of Single Supplier on Customer Business: When a customer's operations are heavily reliant on a single supplier's products or services, the potential business impact if the supplier is discontinued is significant. This data element assesses the degree to which the supplier's products or services affect the customer's core business and highlights the company's market control.

Through the comprehensive analysis of these five data elements, customer dependency can be effectively quantified, shedding light on potential technological barriers and monopolistic risks in the market. This method not only provides systematic, data-driven support for evaluating a company's market position but also offers a quantitative basis for decision-making in antitrust regulation.

Network effects refer to the phenomenon in which the value of a product or service increases as the number of users grows. In markets with network effects, the growth in user numbers not only enhances the attractiveness of a platform but also further strengthens user retention and engagement, creating a positive feedback loop. This effect often provides a significant competitive advantage and establishes technological barriers, making it difficult for new entrants to disrupt the market position of incumbents. To systematically evaluate the intensity of network effects and the technological barriers they create, we focus on the following four core data elements:

User Growth Rate: The user growth rate reflects the platform's ability to attract new users. A rapidly growing user base often serves as the initial driving force behind network effects. By analyzing the user growth rate, we can assess the speed at which network effects are formed and their potential impact on the market.

Changes in Market Share: Market share is an important indicator for evaluating the monopolistic advantages brought by network effects. As the platform's user base increases, a rise in market share is often a direct manifestation of network effects, reflecting the platform's dominant position and its exclusivity within the market.

User Interactions: User interaction is a key mechanism for the realization of network effects. Frequent interactions among users (such as social media engagement, or buying and selling on transactional platforms) can significantly enhance the platform's value and increase user stickiness. Therefore, analyzing user interactions helps quantify the intensity of network effects.

Platform Dependency: Platform dependency measures the extent to which users are invested in the platform and the costs associated with switching to a competing platform. High platform dependency typically indicates that network effects are highly developed, making it difficult for users to transition to competing platforms. This metric reflects the solidity of technological barriers and the potential for monopolistic behavior.

These four data elements—spanning user growth, market performance, user behavior, and platform dependency—provide a multi-dimensional evaluation of the impact of network effects on technological barriers. This comprehensive analysis serves as a foundational framework for subsequent monopolistic risk assessment.

These four categories of data elements—spanning user growth, market behavior, user interactions, and platform dependency—provide a multi-faceted evaluation of how network effects contribute to technological barriers. This analysis forms the basis for a systematic approach to assessing potential monopolistic risks in the marketplace (Table 5.4).

Data control and processing capabilities refer to an enterprise's comprehensive strength in acquiring, integrating, analyzing, and applying data resources. This

Table 5.4 Analysis of data elements related to network effects

Data element	Explanation	Quantitative examples
User growth rate	A metric that measures the rate at which the platform's user base grows over a specific period, typically expressed as a percentage.	**High Risk**: Extremely high growth rate, e.g., annual growth rate exceeding 50%.**Medium Risk**: Moderate growth rate, e.g., annual growth rate between 20%–50%.**Low Risk**: Low growth rate, e.g., annual growth rate below 20%.
Changes in market share	The growth or decline in the platform's market share within the broader market. This metric is usually measured by comparing the market share at the initial and final time points, reflecting the trend in the platform's competitive position.	**High Risk**: Rapid market share growth, e.g., annual increase exceeding 10%.**Medium Risk**: Steady market share growth, e.g., annual increase between 5%–10%.**Low Risk**: Slow or stagnant market share growth, e.g., annual increase below 5%.
User interactions	The frequency and diversity of interactions and transactions among users on the platform, including, but not limited to, messaging, content sharing, reviews, likes, comments, and online transactions. Frequent and diverse interactions typically reflect user engagement and platform health.	**High Risk**: Extremely frequent user interactions, e.g., average user interaction exceeds 10 times per day. **Medium Risk**: Moderate user interaction, e.g., average user interaction between 5–10 times per day. **Low Risk**: Low user interaction, e.g., average user interaction below 5 times per day.
Platform dependency	Measures the proportion and frequency of users who rely on the platform for core activities such as transactions, socializing, or information gathering. High platform dependency reflects strong user engagement and the potential for high switching costs.	**High Risk**: High platform dependency, e.g., over 80% of users report that leaving the platform would significantly affect their activities. **Medium Risk**: Moderate dependency, e.g., 40%–80% of users report some impact if leaving the platform. **Low Risk**: Low dependency, e.g., fewer than 40% of users report that leaving the platform would have a significant impact.

concept encompasses the entire pipeline from extensive data collection to in-depth data mining, efficient processing, and decision-making driven by actionable insights. Evaluating these capabilities is crucial for identifying an enterprise's technological barriers and competitive advantages. Four key data elements serve as assessment metrics (Table 5.5):

Breadth and Depth of Data Collection
The breadth captures the enterprise's ability to encompass a panoramic view of the market, users, and business landscape. Depth represents the granularity and multidimensionality of the data collected. Enterprises with extensive and detailed data collection capabilities can gain comprehensive market insights, enabling rapid strategic adjustments in response to market dynamics and establishing competitive barriers.

Data Processing and Analytical Capability
This metric highlights an enterprise's ability to handle massive datasets efficiently and extract meaningful insights using advanced analytical techniques such as machine learning and deep learning. Superior data processing and analytical capabilities enhance market trend predictions, improve resource allocation, and strengthen strategic decision-making with scientific precision.

Market Impact of Data
This dimension measures the influence of data analysis on enterprise decision-making, focusing on the competitive advantage derived from these insights. Enterprises that effectively use data analysis to guide product positioning, pricing strategies, and user operations often achieve higher market share and stronger industry positioning, thereby creating significant technological barriers.

Data Exclusivity
Data exclusivity reflects the availability and substitutability of critical data resources. Highly exclusive data sources indicate that competitors face significant challenges in obtaining equivalent-quality data, creating notable entry barriers and solidifying the enterprise's dominant market position.

These four categories collectively form a comprehensive framework for evaluating an enterprise's data control and processing capabilities. This framework helps to understand how enterprises leverage data resources to establish technological barriers and competitive advantages within the digital economy. By analyzing these key elements, we can better assess the strategic implications of data-driven practices in fostering innovation and market leadership.

Competitor behavior encompasses the various strategies and actions undertaken by market participants to gain a competitive advantage. These behaviors include pricing strategies, product innovation, market expansion, and customer retention efforts. Such activities not only reflect the competitive dynamics of the market but also reveal the extent to which technological barriers hinder new entrants. To systematically quantify and analyze technological barriers, the following four critical data elements are employed (Table 5.6):

Table 5.5 Analysis of key data elements related to data control and processing capabilities

Element	Explanation	Quantitative examples
Breadth and depth of data collection	Breadth refers to the diversity of data sources (e.g., user behavior data, market transaction data, social media data, sensor data) and the wide coverage of industries, regions, and user groups. Depth reflects the granularity of data mined from individual sources, including aspects such as temporal, sequential, and detailed data attributes. For instance, the depth of user behavior data may include detailed records such as individual click interactions, time spent, and browsing paths.	By the number of data types:—High Risk: Collecting and processing more than 10 data types (e.g., personal profiles, purchase history, browsing behavior, social media interactions). - Medium Risk: Collecting 5–10 data types. - Low Risk: Collecting fewer than 5 data types.
Data Processing and Analytical Capability	This refers to the comprehensive ability of an enterprise to efficiently clean, integrate, transform, and store large-scale, multi-source, and multi-type data. It includes leveraging advanced analytical tools and algorithms (e.g., machine learning, deep learning) to extract valuable insights. Beyond robust computational infrastructure, this capability demands mature data processing workflows and advanced methods to support a wide range of business needs, from real-time decision-making to long-term strategic planning.	By the sophistication of analytical tools: - High Risk: Using advanced analytical tools and techniques (e.g., machine learning, artificial intelligence) for in-depth analysis and prediction. - Medium Risk: Using intermediate tools like SQL queries or advanced Excel functionalities. - Low Risk: Using basic tools like basic Excel functions or traditional statistical methods.
Market Impact of Data	This measures the strategic advantage derived from the enterprise's data resources and their role in driving corporate decisions and market actions. Specifically, it evaluates the extent to which data analytics influence critical decisions, such as business strategy, product positioning, user operations, and pricing.	By the extent of data influence: - High Risk: Analytical results significantly influence market prices, consumer behavior on a large scale, or industry standards. - Medium Risk: Analytics impact a specific field or a small market segment. - Low Risk: Analytics primarily support internal decisions with minimal market impact.
Data Exclusivity	Exclusivity reflects the scarcity and proprietary nature of the data (e.g., user behavior data, proprietary platform transaction data), as well as the unique control enterprises have over data collection channels. Data exclusivity forms a critical barrier in data-driven decision-making, innovation, and market competition, preventing competitors from replicating or acquiring similar data advantages.	By the availability of substitute data sources: - High Risk: The enterprise has near-exclusive access to key data with virtually no substitutes in the market. - Medium Risk: The enterprise controls some critical data, but substitutes exist. - Low Risk: Data is limited, with multiple substitutes available in the market.

Table 5.6 Analysis of data elements related to competitor behavior

Data element	Explanation	Quantitative example
Number of Market Competitors	Refers to the number of enterprises participating in a specific market or industry that provide similar or substitute products and services. This metric measures the market's concentration and competitive dynamics.	**High Risk**: Fewer than 3 major competitors in the market. **Medium Risk**: 3–5 major competitors in the market. **Low Risk**: More than 5 major competitors.
Market Share Distribution	Indicates the size and relative distribution of market share held by competitors in a specific market. Market share is typically based on metrics such as sales revenue, sales volume, or user base, reflecting the proportion of the total market occupied by a specific competitor.	**High Risk**: Top three competitors hold over 70% of the market share. **Medium Risk**: Top three competitors hold 40%–70%.**Low Risk**: Top three hold less than 40%.
Degree of Price Competition Among Competitors	Price competition involves firms reducing the price of their products or services to attract more customers or expand market share in the short term. This strategy can lead to phenomena such as price wars, decreased profit margins, and increased consumer welfare.	**High Risk**: Very limited or no price competition; price changes among major competitors are minimal. **Medium Risk**: Moderate price competition; competitors occasionally adjust prices in response to rivals. **Low Risk**: Intense price competition; competitors frequently adjust prices to attract customers.
Frequency of New Market Entrants	Refers to the frequency with which new participants (typically startups or new business units of existing firms) successfully enter the target market and begin offering relevant products or services within a specified period. This reflects the market's openness and the height of entry barriers.	**High Risk**: Virtually no new entrants, or fewer than 1 per year. **Medium Risk**: Occasional new entrants, with 2–3 per year. **Low Risk**: Market is open to new entrants, with more than 3 per year.

Number of Market Competitors:

The number of competitors directly reflects the competitive dynamics of the market. A larger number of market participants generally indicates lower entry barriers, while a market dominated by only a few firms suggests the presence of significant technological barriers and entry obstacles.

Market Share Distribution:

The concentration of market share is a key indicator of technological barriers. High market share concentration often implies that a few firms possess significant technological advantages, creating substantial entry barriers and making it difficult for new competitors to capture a meaningful share of the market in the short term.

Degree of Price Competition Among Competitors:

The intensity of price competition indicates the level of market competition. Intense price wars often suggest relatively low technological barriers, as firms rely more on price strategies than technological superiority. Conversely, weak price competition may indicate that firms depend on technological monopolies to maintain high profit margins and market dominance.

Frequency of New Market Entrants:
The frequency of new entrants into the market serves as an important measure of entry barriers and market openness. Frequent entry by new firms generally indicates low entry barriers and insufficient technological advantages to establish long-term market obstacles. Conversely, a scarcity of new entrants suggests high technological barriers, with existing firms using technological advantages or patent protections to deter potential competitors.

The above four data elements provide a systematic approach to assessing the impact of technological barriers on market competition. They help identify potential monopolistic behaviors and structural issues within the market, offering quantitative support for antitrust analysis. This framework contributes to a deeper understanding of market dynamics and informs effective regulatory interventions.

Consumer welfare broadly refers to the overall economic benefits consumers derive from the market, encompassing utility, value, and freedom of choice associated with available products or services. A core objective of antitrust analysis is to assess the potential impact of market power on consumer welfare, particularly in cases where monopolistic behavior or market dominance may arise.

To comprehensively evaluate the impact on consumer welfare, it is crucial to construct a framework incorporating four key data elements (Table 5.7):

Changes in Product or Service Prices:
Price levels serve as a direct indicator of consumer welfare. Monopoly or market dominance often results in price increases, undermining consumer interests. Key metrics for evaluating price changes include historical pricing trends, price volatility, and comparisons with similar products, aimed at identifying potential price manipulation or unfair pricing practices.

Changes in Product or Service Quality:
Quality represents a vital component of perceived consumer value and is a critical determinant of consumer welfare. A lack of competition may lead firms to reduce investments in quality, thereby lowering overall product or service standards. Quality metrics can include user feedback scores, product functionality evaluations, and failure rates, enabling assessment of quality deterioration as market concentration increases.

Product or Service Diversity and Innovation:
Competitive markets encourage firms to introduce diverse and innovative products to meet varying consumer needs. Conversely, market dominance may lead to reduced diversity and innovation, narrowing consumer choices. Relevant metrics include the speed of new product launches, the number of product categories, and patent application counts, reflecting the innovation dynamism and diversity levels of the market.

Table 5.7 Analysis of Consumer Welfare-Related Data Elements

Name	Explanation	Quantitative Examples
Changes in Product or Service Prices	The fluctuation of prices for specific products or services in the market over a given period. In antitrust analysis, price changes are a critical focus since unreasonable price increases often result from monopolistic behavior or abuse of market dominance.	**High Risk:** Prices rise consistently over time, exceeding the industry average increase by 50% or more. **Medium Risk:** Prices remain stable or fluctuate mildly, with changes within ±20% of the industry average. **Low Risk:** Prices decrease consistently over time, falling below the industry average decline by 20% or more.
Changes in Product or Service Quality	Quality changes directly impact consumer satisfaction and perceived value. In competitive markets, firms typically improve quality to attract and retain customers. However, in monopolistic markets, firms may reduce investment in quality, leading to declines that harm overall consumer welfare.	**High Risk:** The top three competitors control over 70% of market share. **Medium Risk:** The top three competitors control between 40%-70% of market share. **Low Risk:** The top three competitors control less than 40% of market share.
Product or Service Diversity and Innovation	High diversity often indicates robust market competition, where firms use differentiation strategies to attract various consumer groups. In contrast, under monopolistic or dominant market conditions, diversity may decline, limiting consumer choices.	**High Risk:** A reduction in product/service variety or stagnation in innovation, with the frequency of new product launches less than 50% of the industry average. **Medium Risk:** Product/service variety and innovation levels match the industry average. **Low Risk:** An increase in product/service variety and active innovation, with new product launch frequencies exceeding the industry average by 20% or more.
Degree of Restriction on Consumer Choice	The extent to which consumers face limitations on their choice due to external market forces or corporate behavior. Such restrictions often manifest as reduced access to alternatives or higher acquisition costs, stemming from market entry barriers, product tying, exclusive agreements, or monopolistic dominance.	**High Risk:** Consumers have almost no alternative options, or the cost of accessing alternatives increases by over 50%. **Medium Risk:** Consumers have some alternative options, with access costs comparable to industry averages. **Low Risk:** Consumers have a broad range of alternative options, with access costs falling below industry averages by 20% or more.

Degree of Restriction on Consumer Choice:
Monopolies or dominant market players may employ tactics such as exclusive agreements or tying arrangements to restrict consumer choices, weakening market competition. Metrics for assessing restrictions include market entry barriers, the availability of substitutes, and consumer switching costs, collectively capturing the degree of freedom consumers have in different market environments.

By constructing these four categories of data elements, it is possible to systematically evaluate the multifaceted impact of technological barriers on consumer welfare. This framework provides robust scientific support for antitrust decision-making and market regulation. It captures both explicit impacts, such as changes in prices and quality, and implicit damages, such as declines in innovation and consumer choice, revealing the comprehensive effects of market failure on consumer welfare.

The regulatory environment is a crucial reference for understanding monopolistic behavior and assessing the risk levels associated with it. It refers to the intensity and efficiency of government and institutional oversight of market competition, directly influencing corporate behavior and market structures. Regulatory environments can be classified into three levels based on their rigor and effectiveness:

- **High-Risk Environment**:
- This environment is characterized by lax regulation with limited constraints on monopolistic practices. Due to insufficient investment in market oversight and antitrust enforcement, firms may exploit regulatory gaps to reinforce their market position through price manipulation, exclusive agreements, and other tactics. Such an environment further weakens market competition, increases market concentration, and poses significant threats to consumer welfare.
- **Medium-Risk Environment**:
- In this scenario, regulatory bodies exhibit moderate levels of market oversight, but enforcement may be limited by resource constraints or low prioritization. While antitrust laws and regulations exist, their implementation may be inconsistent. Firms face some regulatory pressure but may still exploit strategic loopholes to gain competitive advantages. This environment may result in modest increases in market concentration while retaining some degree of competition.
- **Low-Risk Environment**:
- A low-risk regulatory environment reflects stringent antitrust oversight and efficient enforcement. Regulatory bodies operate within well-defined legal frameworks and effectively monitor market dynamics, intervening promptly when necessary. In such an environment, corporate behavior is strictly controlled, reducing the risk of market abuse and fostering fair competition, consumer protection, and innovation.

This expanded analysis highlights the critical role of regulatory environments in shaping market dynamics and protecting consumer welfare, emphasizing the need for robust enforcement mechanisms to mitigate the risks associated with monopolistic behavior.

5.2 Design of an Intelligent System for Computational Antitrust

5.2.1 System Requirements and Functional Analysis

With the rapid development of the digital economy, market competition has grown increasingly complex. Monopolistic behaviors are becoming more concealed, diversified, and digitized, rendering traditional antitrust regulatory methods insufficient to meet the demands of this new era. In response, the development of an intelligent system for computational antitrust has become imperative. Such a system supports antitrust enforcement agencies in efficiently and precisely identifying and monitoring potential monopolistic behaviors in the digital economy. This section analyzes system requirements and functional design, incorporating the application of large models to outline the core functional modules and technological supports of the intelligent computational antitrust system.

5.2.1.1 System Requirements Analysis

Data Collection and Integration

The intelligent system must efficiently collect and integrate market data from diverse sources, including transactional data, market share data, social media insights, and publicly available financial reports. The data collection process must prioritize privacy protection and data security, ensuring compliance with legal and regulatory frameworks.

Detection of Monopolistic Behaviors

The system requires large-scale data processing and the ability to identify monopolistic behaviors. It should handle extensive, heterogeneous datasets through cleaning, preprocessing, and real-time analysis. By leveraging advanced algorithms, such as data mining, machine learning, and deep learning, the system must detect potential monopolistic practices, including price discrimination, market foreclosure, and exclusive agreements.

Flexible Model Development and Iteration

Given the dynamic and complex nature of monopolistic behaviors, the system must support flexible model development and rapid iteration. Specifically, it should provide a comprehensive library of modeling tools and an extensible framework to support both traditional economic models (e.g., regression analysis, Granger causality analysis) and modern machine learning models (e.g., decision trees, graph neural networks, time-series forecasting, and large models).

Real-Time Monitoring and Alerts

The system must continuously monitor market dynamics and enterprise behaviors, using intelligent algorithms to automatically identify anomalies. Upon detecting potential monopolistic risks or abnormal market behaviors, the system should issue timely alerts and generate detailed reports for regulatory reference.

Interpretability and Compliance
To meet regulatory requirements, the system must offer interpretability in its analysis processes. It should provide transparent explanations for model outputs and employ detailed metrics analysis and visualization to help regulatory personnel understand decision-making rationales. This avoids uncertainties arising from "black-box" algorithms.

Application of Large Models
With the advancement of large language models (LLMs) and multimodal models, the system must incorporate these technologies to enhance its understanding of text and multimodal data. Specifically, in analyzing unstructured data such as corporate communications, market reports, and public sentiment, large models can significantly improve semantic analysis, sentiment detection, and pattern recognition capabilities.

5.2.1.2 System Functional Analysis

Data Management and Storage Module
This module is responsible for storing and managing diverse data types, including structured data (e.g., database records), semi-structured data (e.g., JSON files), and unstructured data (e.g., text and images). It must support efficient indexing and querying to enable rapid data retrieval and analysis.

Analysis and Modeling Module
As the core functional module of the system, this module handles data analysis and model building. It should incorporate a variety of economic analysis tools and state-of-the-art machine learning algorithms, enabling quantitative and predictive analyses. The module must also dynamically adjust model parameters based on market changes to improve the accuracy and flexibility of its analyses.

Risk Identification and Alert Module
This module leverages machine learning and data mining technologies to identify potential monopolistic behaviors and risks. By analyzing market transaction data and behavioral patterns of enterprises, it can generate risk scores and provide real-time alerts for high-risk entities and activities.

Visualization and Report Generation Module
The visualization module employs graphical and data presentation techniques to help users intuitively understand market dynamics and analysis results. It should support a variety of visualization methods, such as time-series graphs, heatmaps, and relationship diagrams. Additionally, the system must automatically generate comprehensive analysis reports, including detailed data analysis results, risk assessments, and regulatory recommendations for decision-makers.

Compliance and Audit Module
The compliance module ensures that data collection, analysis, and model application comply with relevant legal and regulatory requirements. The audit module records operational logs and analysis decisions, enabling post-hoc reviews and compliance verification.

System Management and User Interface Module

The system must provide a user-friendly management interface and user access control, supporting multi-role access and permissions. Administrators can configure data sources, adjust detection models, and view analysis reports, while users can access market analysis and case investigation results according to their permissions (Fig. 5.1).

By significantly enhancing the efficiency and precision of antitrust enforcement, the intelligent system for computational antitrust offers innovative technical solutions to safeguard fair competition in the digital economy. This contributes to building a healthier and more orderly market competition ecosystem).

5.2.2 System Technical Architecture

This system adopts an architecture that integrates frontend-backend separation with a deeply integrated antitrust large model. It provides comprehensive support for the entire workflow, from data collection to the identification and visualization of

Fig. 5.1 Computational Antitrust Intelligent System Design

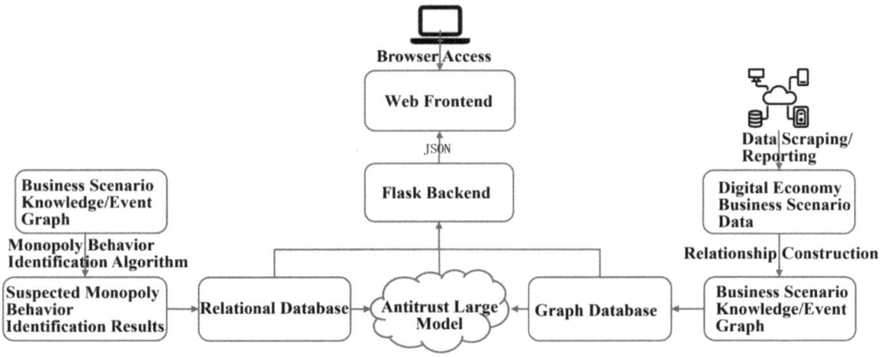

Fig. 5.2 Technical Architecture of the Computational Antitrust Intelligent System

monopolistic behavior. The system architecture, illustrated in Fig. 5.2, is designed with modularity to achieve high scalability, robust performance, and ease of maintenance, accommodating the complex requirements of antitrust scenarios.

5.2.2.1 Frontend Design

The frontend handles direct user interaction, including functions for data upload, results display, and visual analytics. Built with the Vue.js framework, the frontend leverages its component-based design to enable efficient page rendering and dynamic interactions. It communicates with the backend via HTTP requests supporting GET, POST, PUT, and DELETE methods to transmit and update data. To enhance user experience, the frontend integrates visualization tools such as ECharts and D3.js, offering multidimensional and multi-layered data displays, including knowledge graphs, bar charts, line charts, and heatmaps. The frontend design emphasizes responsive layouts to ensure optimal display across various devices.

5.2.2.2 Backend Implementation

The backend is responsible for data processing, business logic implementation, and integration with the antitrust large model. Developed using the Flask framework, the backend exposes RESTful APIs to the frontend, with JSON as the standardized data transmission format. Core functionalities of the backend include data preprocessing, knowledge graph construction, monopolistic behavior detection, and model inference. To support complex antitrust scenarios, the backend employs a flexible task scheduling mechanism and a modular architecture, enabling dynamic extension of functional modules based on business requirements.

5.2.2.3 Data Layer and Knowledge Representation

Data forms the foundation of the system, covering collection, storage, and management. The system supports two primary data sources: user-uploaded business data and web-scraped domestic and international antitrust information. After data acquisition, processes such as cleaning, denoising, and format conversion are performed to prepare the data for subsequent analysis.

The system uses knowledge graph technology to model relationships among events and data elements in business scenarios, providing a digital representation of logical connections within the domain. These knowledge graphs are stored in graph databases like Neo4j, serving as the basis for monopolistic behavior detection and fine-tuning of the antitrust large model. Detection results and associated statistical data are stored in relational databases such as PostgreSQL. Relational databases manage structured data efficiently and support subsequent statistical analysis and querying.

5.2.2.4 Algorithms and Methods for Monopolistic Behavior Detection

The system employs a combination of machine learning, data mining, and economic analysis techniques to enable efficient detection of monopolistic behavior. For various types of monopolistic behavior—such as discriminatory pricing, "choose one of two," and self-preferential practices—the system implements customized detection algorithms. For instance, clustering and classification models are used to detect price discrimination, graph neural networks analyze selective trading relationships between enterprises, and economic indicators quantify market monopoly risks. Verified results are stored in the relational database for further use.

5.2.2.5 Antitrust Large Model Integration

The antitrust large model is a critical component, offering powerful reasoning capabilities and decision-making support. Building on the knowledge graph constructed at the data layer, the large model performs further analysis of complex relationships and generates high-quality inference results. These results are integrated with data from the graph and relational databases through the backend and are presented to the frontend for unified visualization.

5.2.2.6 Unified Visualization and Reporting

The system consolidates statistical results from the graph database, detection outcomes from the relational database, and inference results from the large model, presenting them to the frontend for display. Users can intuitively view the structure of knowledge graphs, detection results for monopolistic behavior, and detailed analytical reports through the frontend interface. To support a wider range of applications, the system also provides multilingual support and customizable report generation.

5.2.2.7 Deployment and Scalability

For deployment and scalability, the system utilizes containerization technologies such as Docker and orchestration tools like Kubernetes, enabling high-availability deployment across cloud environments. Its modular design facilitates the seamless integration of new functional modules, such as domain-specific monopolistic behavior analysis or customized regional market detection. To adapt to potential changes in antitrust regulations, the system can dynamically update rule libraries and fine-tune the large model, ensuring quick and effective compliance.

This architecture ensures the system's adaptability, efficiency, and robustness, meeting the demanding needs of antitrust analysis in the digital economy.

5.2.3 Construction and Integration of Large Models for Computational Antitrust

In the modern economic environment, antitrust regulation faces increasingly complex and diverse challenges. With the continuous evolution of market structures and the explosive growth of data, traditional antitrust analysis methods struggle to meet the demands of efficient and precise regulation. To address these challenges, we propose a methodology for constructing and integrating large computational antitrust models based on advanced natural language processing (NLP) technologies. This approach aims to enhance the efficiency and effectiveness of antitrust regulation through intelligent solutions.

5.2.3.1 Model Construction with LoRA Technology

Our computational antitrust model leverages **Low-Rank Adaptation (LoRA)**, an efficient parameter-tuning method that significantly reduces the number of parameters required for fine-tuning while preserving the original performance of the model. LoRA introduces low-rank adaptation matrices into pre-trained large-scale language models, enabling the efficient integration of domain-specific knowledge without extensive adjustments to the entire model. This capability allows us to rapidly build large models enriched with deep antitrust domain expertise, even with limited computational resources.

The construction process begins with selecting a pre-trained large model with robust language understanding and generation capabilities, such as **GPT-4**. We then fine-tune the model using antitrust-specific domain knowledge. A substantial corpus comprising antitrust-related literature, case analyses, policy documents, and regulatory texts is compiled for this purpose. By conducting targeted training, the model is equipped to better understand and generate content related to antitrust, resulting in higher levels of expertise and accuracy in practical applications.

5.2.3.2 Integration with Intelligent Antitrust Systems

The fine-tuned computational antitrust model is not deployed as a standalone tool but is integrated into an intelligent antitrust system via **API interfaces**. This integration provides high flexibility and scalability, allowing the model's powerful capabilities to be embedded into various antitrust application scenarios.

For instance, in **antitrust public opinion analysis**, the model processes multi-source data from social media, news reports, and other platforms via API calls. It can automatically identify and analyze potential monopolistic behaviors and market anomalies. By understanding complex linguistic expressions and capturing subtle market dynamics, the model provides regulators with real-time, precise monitoring and alerts.

5.2.3.3 Automated Risk Reporting

The computational antitrust model also enables the automatic generation of **monopoly risk assessment reports**. Traditional report generation often relies on manual drafting, which is time-consuming and prone to subjective biases, leading to inconsistencies in objectivity and quality. By leveraging the model's natural language generation capabilities, structured and detailed reports can be automatically created based on input data such as market metrics, policy regulations, and case analyses. These reports not only include key market indicators and analysis results but also offer tailored regulatory recommendations based on different risk levels, significantly improving efficiency and quality.

5.2.3.4 Technical Implementation and Security Considerations

The integration and application of the computational antitrust model involve multiple technical processes. First, **API interface design** must ensure efficient and stable data transmission and model invocation. To achieve this, we employ a modern microservices architecture, deploying the large model on cloud servers and enabling real-time responsiveness via **RESTful APIs** or **gRPC communication protocols**. Whether for real-time public opinion analysis or batch report generation, the system can quickly invoke the model's functionalities to meet various application needs.

Second, strict measures are implemented to ensure **data security and privacy** during API access and data transmission. These include API key authentication, encrypted data transmission, and access logging to safeguard antitrust data throughout its lifecycle. A flexible **permission management mechanism** is also designed to accommodate diverse application needs, allowing different users or departments to access appropriate functionalities within their authorization scope.

5.2.3.5 Practical Applications and Future Adaptability

Through seamless integration with intelligent systems, the computational antitrust model provides comprehensive support for antitrust regulation. For example, during investigations, regulators can submit requests via a user-friendly interface, which triggers the system to invoke the model for data analysis and risk evaluation. Detailed investigation reports are generated automatically, enabling regulators, even without advanced technical expertise, to access professional and accurate results efficiently. This significantly enhances productivity and decision-making quality.

Moreover, the applications of the computational antitrust model are not limited to current regulatory tasks. Its adaptability and extensibility allow it to address emerging regulatory needs and phenomena in new markets. By conducting further fine-tuning and optimization, the model can be updated and enhanced to remain at the forefront of antitrust regulation technology.

In summary, the construction and integration of large models for computational antitrust represent a transformative approach to addressing the challenges of modern regulatory environments. By combining advanced NLP techniques with domain-specific expertise, this methodology enables intelligent, efficient, and adaptive regulatory support, pushing the boundaries of traditional antitrust enforcement.

5.3 Functional Demonstration of the Computational Antitrust Intelligent System

5.3.1 Statistical Analysis and Visualization

Using the digital scenarios in the mobility sector constructed in Chap. 4 as an example, the market share distribution illustrated in Fig. 5.3 provides a clear depiction of the competitive landscape in this industry. The top three companies collectively account for approximately 88% of the market share, while the bottom three companies hold a combined share of only about 12%. This data reveals the preliminary formation of a highly concentrated market. The leading three enterprises typically possess superior financial strength, well-established brand equity, and extensive resource integration capabilities, giving them significant advantages in dynamic pricing, service innovation, and leveraging economies of scale. These strengths not

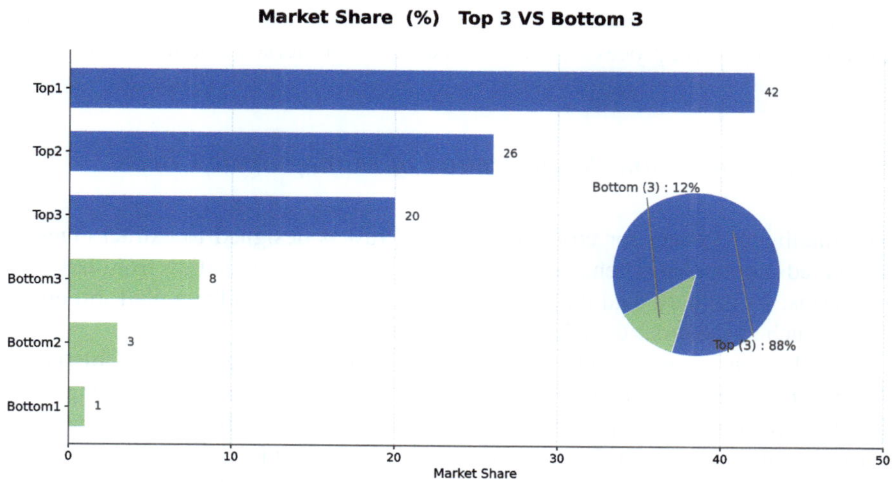

Fig. 5.3 Market Share Analysis

only help them solidify their positions in existing markets but also lay the groundwork for exploring emerging niche markets and pursuing cross-regional expansion.

However, such a market structure, where dominance is concentrated among a few leading enterprises, may pose potential challenges to the industry's overall dynamism over the medium to long term. With the bottom three companies holding only 12% of the market share, smaller businesses and new entrants face considerable survival pressures in terms of pricing negotiations, customer retention, and the pace of technological innovation. For the industry as a whole, this imbalance may hinder the effective operation of diversified competitive mechanisms, making it difficult for emerging business models and differentiated services to thrive due to a lack of sufficient market space. High market concentration enhances the ability of leading enterprises to shape industry standards and dominate discourse, potentially jeopardizing the long-term healthy development of market competition.

From an economic perspective, this situation presents a dual-edged sword. On one hand, large enterprises in highly concentrated markets can leverage economies of scale and establish unified standards, delivering relatively stable prices and predictable service quality to consumers. On the other hand, overly concentrated market structures may evolve into quasi-monopolies or confer significant market dominance, which could weaken consumer choice diversity and disrupt the healthy interaction among suppliers.

By utilizing the precise analyses and data-driven insights of computational antitrust intelligent systems, regulators and policymakers can anticipate subtle structural changes within industries and provide timely, measured guidance. This approach offers the potential to balance the efficient functioning of markets with the encouragement of new entrants. In specific contexts, moderate policy interventions—such as lowering market entry barriers, promoting technology sharing, or strengthening data compliance—could help less dominant enterprises find avenues for survival and innovation. Over the long term, such measures could enhance the dynamic competitive processes of the market and foster its sustainable development.

5.3.2 Discovery and Identification of Monopolistic Clues

The intelligent system for computational antitrust is designed to extract clues of suspected monopolistic behavior from massive datasets originating from business platforms. Its primary data input consists of operational data from platform enterprises, such as the order data framework outlined in Chap. 4.

Initially, the system applies the proposed **Dual Pricing Model Clustering (DPMC)** algorithm to identify orders indicative of discriminatory pricing. The DPMC algorithm plays a pivotal role in this process, effectively filtering patterns of price discrimination from large volumes of order data and conducting clustering analysis. By leveraging this algorithm, the system can uncover potential discriminatory pricing behaviors hidden within complex transactional datasets.

Subsequently, the system constructs a **knowledge graph** of discriminatory pricing behaviors based on the extracted order information. This graph not only details individual orders but also links them to relevant platform enterprises and consumer profiles, as illustrated in Fig. 5.4. By visualizing these connections, the knowledge graph reveals the relationships between discriminatory pricing behaviors, platform enterprises, and affected consumers, providing a rich data foundation for further investigation and analysis.

5.3.2.1 Analysis of Enterprise and Order Distributions

The system proceeds with an in-depth analysis of the enterprises associated with discriminatory pricing behaviors and their respective order distributions. For example, as shown in Fig. 5.5a, the analysis examines the distribution of discriminatory pricing behaviors across various platform enterprises, identifying which companies are more likely to engage in discriminatory pricing strategies. This evaluation not only sheds light on the prevalence of such behaviors but also highlights specific enterprises that may pose potential risks.

5.3.2.2 Consumer-Centric Analysis

In addition to enterprise analysis, the system delves deeply into consumer information from multiple dimensions. As illustrated in Fig. 5.5b, it analyzes consumer characteristics such as occupation, income level, average monthly ride-hailing frequency, and registration duration on the platform. Findings indicate that consumers subjected to discriminatory pricing are predominantly in the **middle-income bracket**, with an average platform registration period of approximately **150 days**.

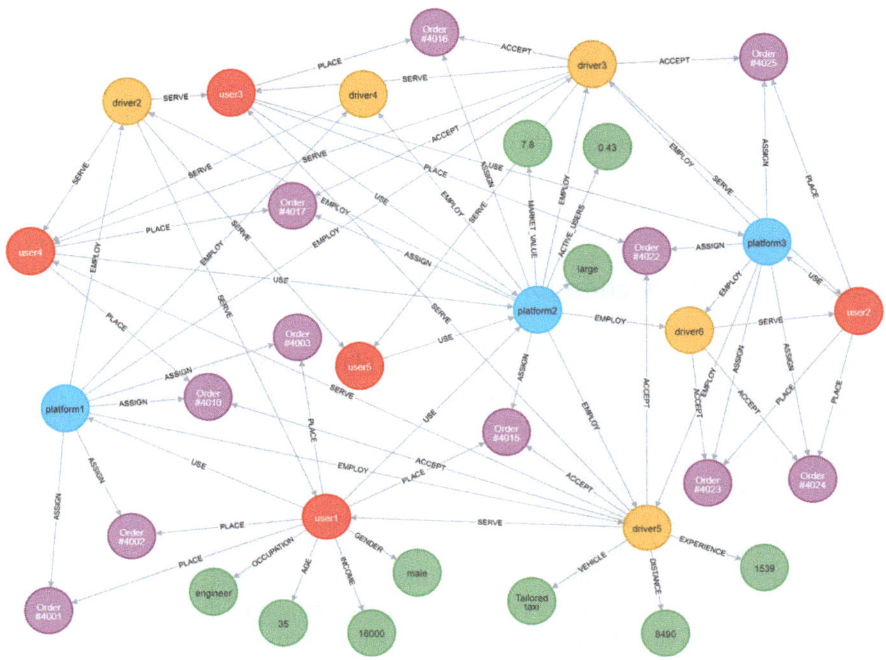

Fig. 5.4 Discriminatory Pricing Behavior Knowledge Graph

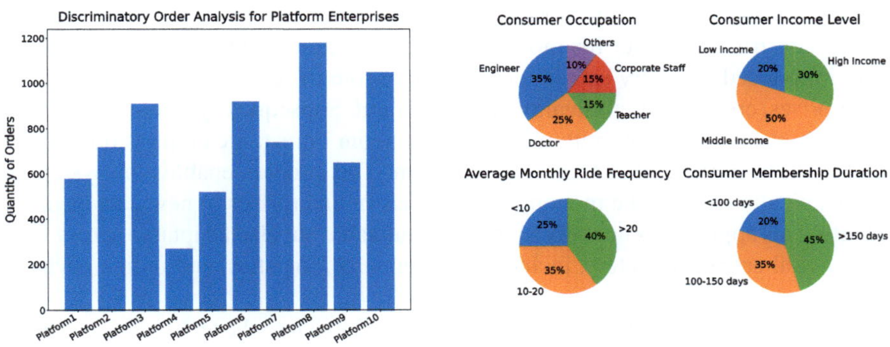

Fig. 5.5 Discriminatory Pricing Behavior Analysis

These insights provide crucial leads for identifying and tracking discriminatory pricing behaviors and offer valuable data support for regulatory bodies aiming to enhance consumer protection.

The module for discovering and identifying monopolistic behavior not only enables the system to extract clues from massive datasets but also facilitates deeper analysis to uncover the underlying factors driving discriminatory pricing and its impact on consumers. Through intelligent processing and precise analytics, this system significantly enhances the efficiency and accuracy of antitrust monitoring, equipping regulators and researchers with robust tools to combat unfair market practices.

This systematic approach ensures that the identification of monopolistic behaviors is not only data-driven but also actionable, paving the way for a more equitable digital economy.

5.3.3 Trend Prediction for Suspected Monopoly Risk Levels

In the context of the rapid development of the platform economy, the structure of market competition has become increasingly complex, and the covert and dynamic nature of monopolistic behavior has significantly intensified. Conducting risk-level trend predictions for monopoly behaviors in platform enterprises can help regulatory agencies identify companies with high monopoly risks from massive datasets, allowing for the early detection of potential issues. Such predictive capabilities enhance the foresight and accuracy of regulatory efforts and provide critical data support for devising scientifically sound intervention strategies. This ensures fair market competition and promotes the healthy development of the digital economy.

Based on the monopoly risk-level data elements discussed in Sect. 5.1.2, digital features such as market share and market concentration of platform enterprises are critical for assessing their monopoly risk. These features are derived from a comprehensive analysis of transaction volumes, user activity, and pricing behavior, reflecting a company's competitive position within the market.

To construct a dataset for monopoly risk levels, an expert scoring mechanism was introduced. Industry experts evaluate and score the comprehensive features of enterprises, creating a high-quality labeled dataset. Subsequently, classical machine learning classification algorithms, such as Random Forest, are employed to model and learn from the expert scoring mechanism. This process enables the system to automatically classify the monopoly risk levels of enterprises in new data environments. This approach is not only highly generalizable but also adaptable across various digital economy sectors, including e-commerce, logistics, and online payment services.

It is worth noting that this discussion does not delve into the technical implementation details of specific machine learning algorithms. Instead, it emphasizes their application in constructing intelligent early warning systems. This framework, combining expert knowledge and machine learning, provides regulatory agencies with a systematic and scientific tool to significantly enhance regulatory efficiency.

Figure 5.6 illustrates the monopoly risk levels for platform enterprises A, B, and C across different months. From the figure, the trends in risk levels are evident. For example, Enterprise A exhibited a low risk level at the beginning of the year, which escalated rapidly to a medium-high risk zone mid-year. Enterprise B's risk level initially decreased before rising again, while Enterprise C showed a significant decline in risk level towards the end of the year. These trends serve as clear signals

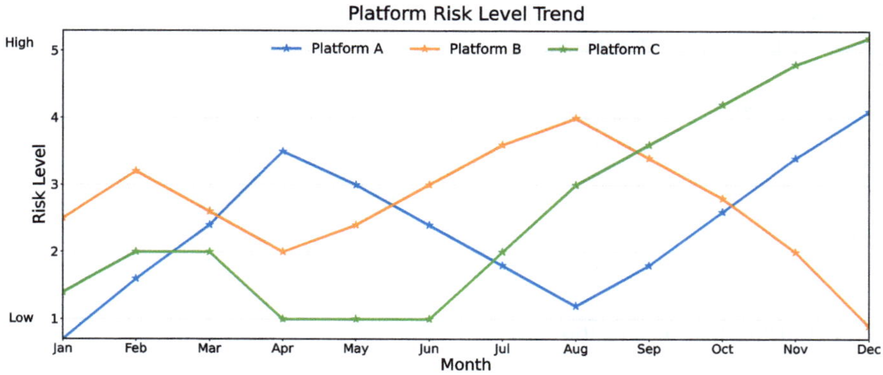

Fig. 5.6 Risk Level Trends

for regulatory agencies, highlighting specific periods when enterprises with high monopoly risks require closer attention.

By analyzing these trends, regulatory agencies can further investigate the underlying drivers of enterprise behavior. For instance, significant changes in market share might indicate unfair competition, or fluctuations in market concentration might reflect risks associated with industry consolidation. By integrating dynamic data with risk prediction models, regulatory efforts can shift from traditional reactive interventions to proactive early warnings and dynamic monitoring.

5.3.4 Intelligent Generation of Monopoly Risk Assessment Reports

To enhance regulatory efficiency, this system leverages the powerful data analysis and generative capabilities of computational antitrust large models to automatically generate assessment reports focused on key enterprises and the competitive environment of specific industries. This functionality allows antitrust regulators to identify potential monopolistic behaviors more accurately and promptly, while also enabling in-depth analysis of the competitive dynamics within businesses and markets. The report generation process is primarily based on multi-dimensional information integration and analysis conducted by the system.

Firstly, the reports automatically identify and extract critical clues related to suspected monopolistic behaviors, as derived from the findings in Chap. 4 on monopoly clue identification and detection. These clues encompass, but are not limited to, corporate pricing strategies, price discrimination, and other relevant practices, providing a robust data foundation for subsequent risk assessments. Subsequently, the system refines the evaluation results by referencing the key data elements of risk level assessments outlined in Sect. 5.1.3, such as market share and industry concentration ratios.

Com_Anti_v1:latest
[Platform Disconnection Risk Rating Report]

1. Introduction

To deeply analyze the current competitive landscape of the market and identify potential disconnection risks, this report provides a comprehensive quantitative and qualitative assessment of three representative internet platforms based on data analysis. Through a combined method of quantification and qualitative judgment, we aim to determine each enterprise's positioning in the market and the likelihood of disconnection risk.

2. Data Dimensions and Indicators

1. **User Scale**: Evaluates the difficulty of attracting and retaining users on the platform.
2. **Market Share**: Calculates the platform's share in its core business domain.
3. **Revenue Source Diversity**: Analyzes whether the enterprise relies on a single or a few revenue streams.
4. **Innovation Capability and Technological Edge**: Assesses the enterprise's investment in R&D, innovation strength, and technological leadership in the industry.

3. Platform Data Analysis

1. Platform A

- **User Scale**: 200 million monthly active users
- **Market Share**: 30%
- **Revenue Source Diversity**: Medium (mainly dependent on advertising revenue)
- **Innovation Capability and Technological Edge**: Strong, especially in big data analytics

Evaluation Result:
Platform A has significant market influence and ↓ ng technological innovation capabilities.
P
询问任何问题

Fig. 5.7 Report Generation Based on Computational Antitrust Large Model

Furthermore, the report generation process incorporates the results of suspected monopoly risk level predictions discussed in Sect. 5.3.3. This component utilizes machine learning algorithms trained on historical data to forecast the monopoly risk levels of enterprises. Based on these predictions, the system integrates critical factors such as company size, technological innovation capabilities, and market share, while also considering the overall competitive landscape of the industry. This comprehensive analysis results in the generation of a detailed and thorough monopoly risk assessment report.

For instance, Fig. 5.7 presents an assessment report for Company A. The report not only lists Company A's market share and user base size but also delves into the company's technological innovation capacity and its competitive position within the industry. By combining big data analytics, machine learning algorithms, and the essence of antitrust regulations, these intelligently generated assessment reports enable regulators to make informed decisions and judgments from multiple dimensions and perspectives.

5.3.5 Exploring Interdepartmental Collaboration

The core of interdepartmental collaboration lies in information sharing, which not only enhances the operational efficiency of various departments but also enables a more refined and comprehensive regulatory mechanism in antitrust oversight. Through effective information sharing, interdepartmental coordination can leverage big data to respond swiftly, formulate more rational policies, and safeguard fair market competition.

Taking the field of mobile transportation as an example, a typical application scenario of interdepartmental collaboration involves real-time data analysis and information sharing to optimize urban traffic management. In such cases, various departments—such as traffic management, urban planning, and antitrust regulatory authorities—need to share and coordinate data from multiple sources to achieve mutually beneficial governance outcomes. For instance, in Beijing, big data from ride-hailing platforms can generate real-time heatmaps of trip origins, as illustrated in Fig. 5.8. This visualization intuitively reveals areas with dense trip demand, particularly highlighted in red zones, which reflect regions with high travel needs.

Fig. 5.8 Heatmap of Order Distribution Across Different Regions in Beijing

The sharing of such information is invaluable not only to ride-hailing platforms but also to traffic management departments, providing critical data support. Leveraging this data, relevant departments can optimize dispatch strategies, adjust vehicle distribution, and deploy transportation resources more efficiently. They can also rationally plan public transit routes to better meet user demand. Furthermore, antitrust regulatory authorities can use this data to analyze whether market distortions—such as price manipulation or service exclusivity—are present. For example, if a particular ride-hailing platform monopolizes high-demand areas, risks such as price manipulation or service quality degradation may arise. Identifying and regulating these potential monopolistic behaviors require interdepartmental cooperation.

Moreover, interdepartmental collaboration can alleviate traffic pressures and reduce urban congestion and environmental pollution. Supported by shared real-time data, traffic management departments can not only predict travel demand but also implement more flexible response measures. For example, by integrating real-time traffic flow data, these departments can dynamically adjust traffic signal timings, optimize traffic patterns, or deploy shared mobility services in high-demand areas. This approach helps distribute the load on public transportation systems, mitigating congestion and improving overall urban mobility.

Such collaborative efforts exemplify how interdepartmental coordination, empowered by advanced data-sharing technologies, can achieve synergistic benefits for urban governance, fair competition, and sustainable development.

5.4 Chapter Summary

This chapter primarily focuses on the development of a risk assessment and early warning system for monopolistic behavior. It establishes a comprehensive framework for evaluating the risks associated with monopolistic practices and introduces a machine learning-based method for risk identification through the analysis of data elements and the construction of risk levels. The chapter begins by identifying the various types of monopolistic behaviors and analyzes the components of risk levels from multiple perspectives, ultimately forming a multidimensional risk assessment framework. Furthermore, it proposes the design of a computational antitrust intelligent system, combining bottom-up and top-down architectural principles. This system introduces a large-scale antitrust model that encompasses the entire process, from data collection to model integration.

In terms of system functionality, this chapter presents several key features of the intelligent antitrust system. These include statistical analysis and visualization of monopolistic behaviors, proactive detection and identification of potential clues, global public opinion analysis, and intelligent clue recommendation. The system is also equipped with advanced knowledge inference capabilities, enabling it to predict trends in the risk levels associated with suspected monopolistic practices. Additionally, by generating intelligent risk assessment reports, the system provides real-time evaluations and actionable strategies to regulatory authorities, significantly enhancing the efficiency of antitrust monitoring and enforcement.

This chapter lays the groundwork for integrating computational methodologies into antitrust efforts, demonstrating the potential of intelligent systems to transform regulatory practices through advanced data-driven insights and decision-making tools.

References

1. Relkar AS (2021) Risk analysis of equipment failure through failure mode and effect analysis and fault tree analysis. J Failure Anal Preven 21:793–805
2. Curti F, Gerlach J, Kazinnik S. (2023) Cyber risk definition and classification for financial risk management. J Operat Risk
3. Prs Group (2011) International country risk guide methodology. PRS Group, East Syracuse, NY
4. Zhuang YY, Wei H (2023) Early warning model and prevention of regional financial risk integrated into legal system. PLos One 18(6):e0286685

MIX
Papier aus verantwortungsvollen Quellen
Paper from responsible sources
FSC® C105338

If you have any concerns about our products,
you can contact us on
ProductSafety@springernature.com

In case Publisher is established outside the EU,
the EU authorized representative is:
Springer Nature Customer Service Center GmbH
Europaplatz 3, 69115 Heidelberg, Germany

Printed by Libri Plureos GmbH
in Hamburg, Germany